# GREAT DISASTERS

# HURRICANES

**Other books in the Great Disasters series:**

# GREAT DISASTERS

DISCARD

# HURRICANES

Mary E. Williams, *Book Editor*

Daniel Leone, *President*
Bonnie Szumski, *Publisher*
Scott Barbour, *Managing Editor*

GREENHAVEN
PRESS®

THOMSON
———✶———™
GALE

San Diego • Detroit • New York • San Francisco • Cleveland
New Haven, Conn. • Waterville, Maine • London • Munich

# THOMSON

✳ ™

## GALE

| LIBRARY OF CONGRESS CATALOGING-IN-PUBLICATION DATA |
| --- |
| Hurricanes / Mary E. Williams, book editor. |
|    p. cm. — (Great disasters) |
| Includes bibliographical references and index. |
|    ISBN 0-7377-1444-1 (pbk. : alk. paper) — ISBN 0-7377-1443-3 (lib. : alk. paper) |
|     1. Hurricanes. I. Williams, Mary E., 1960–  . II. Great disasters (Greenhaven Press) |
| QC944.F56  2004 |
| 363.34'922—dc21                                   2003049137 |

# CONTENTS

## Chapter 1: The Science and Study of Hurricanes

### 1. The Nature of Hurricanes
*by David E. Fisher*
Though hurricanes are infamous for their destructive
winds, it is the storm surge—a massive wind-driven
wave—that causes the greatest loss of life.

### 2. Predicting the Intensity of Hurricanes
*by Robert Henson*
Meteorologists find it difficult to forecast the strength
of hurricanes. This is partly due to a lack of critical
atmospheric and oceanic data in the tropics. Innova-
tions in satellite technology and observational tools
offer hope for more accurate predictions in the
future.

### 3. Hurricanes and Global Warming
*by David Bjerklie and Dick Thompson*
Scientists warn that global warming could bring
about stronger hurricanes in the twenty-first century.
Yet several other factors—such as wind and sea currents and alternating El Niño and La Niña conditions—may counterbalance the hurricane-producing
potential of global warming.

### 4. Hunting Prehistoric Hurricanes
*by John Tarvis*
Paleotempestology—the study of prehistoric hurricanes—is a relatively new field that may help clima-
tologists estimate the frequency of future hurricanes.
Researchers in this field examine lake bed sediments,
coral skeletons, and tree rings to document ancient
cyclones.

# Chapter 2: Disasters and Personal Accounts

was buffeted by severe turbulence in Hugo's eye
wall—the most dangerous part of a hurricane.

# Chapter 3: Preventing Calamity

### 1. Improving Hurricane Forecasting
*by Richard A. Kerr*
Global Positioning System satellite technology and
improved computer modeling are allowing scientists
to more accurately predict a hurricane's storm track.
More precise forecasting means that averting disaster
will be cheaper and less disruptive in the future.

### 2. A Guide to Hurricane Preparedness
*by the National Oceanic and Atmospheric Administration*
A government agency provides information on hurricane preparedness and safety that can help those
affected protect themselves and their property.

# FOREWORD

Humans have an ambivalent relationship with their home planet, nurtured on the one hand by Earth's bounty but devastated on the other hand by its catastrophic natural disasters. While these events are the results of the natural processes of Earth, their consequences for humans frequently include the disastrous destruction of lives and property. For example, when the volcanic island of Krakatau exploded in 1883, the eruption generated vast seismic sea waves called tsunamis that killed about thirty-six thousand people in Indonesia. In a single twenty-four-hour period in the United States in 1974, at least 148 tornadoes carved paths of death and destruction across thirteen states. In 1976, an earthquake completely destroyed the industrial city of Tangshan, China, killing more than 250,000 residents.

Some natural disasters have gone beyond relatively localized destruction to completely alter the course of human history. Archaeological evidence suggests that one of the greatest natural disasters in world history happened in A.D. 535, when an Indonesian "supervolcano" exploded near the same site where Krakatau arose later. The dust and debris from this gigantic eruption blocked the light and heat of the sun for eighteen months, radically altering weather patterns around the world and causing crop failure in Asia and the Middle East. Rodent populations increased with the weather changes, causing an epidemic of bubonic plague that decimated entire populations in Africa and Europe. The most powerful volcanic eruption in recorded human history also happened in Indonesia. When the volcano Tambora erupted in 1815, it ejected an estimated 1.7 million tons of debris in an explosion that was heard more than a thousand miles away and that continued to rumble for three months. Atmospheric dust from the eruption blocked much of the sun's heat, producing what was called "the year without summer" and creating worldwide climatic havoc, starvation, and disease.

As these examples illustrate, natural disasters can have as much impact on human societies as the bloodiest wars and most chaotic political revolutions. Therefore, they are as worthy of study as the major events of world history. As with the study of social and political events, the exploration of natural disasters can illuminate the causes of these catastrophes and target the lessons learned about how to mitigate and prevent the loss of life when disaster strikes again. By examining these events and the forces behind them, the Greenhaven Press Great Disasters series is designed to help students better understand such cataclysmic events. Each anthology in the series focuses on a specific type of natural disaster or a particular disastrous event in history. An introductory essay provides a general overview of the subject of the anthology, placing natural disasters in historical and scientific context. The essays that follow, written by specialists in the field, researchers, journalists, witnesses, and scientists, explore the science and nature of natural disasters, describing particular disasters in detail and discussing related issues, such as predicting, averting, or managing disasters. To aid the reader in choosing appropriate material, each essay is preceded by a concise summary of its content and biographical information about its author.

In addition, each volume contains extensive material to help the student researcher. An annotated table of contents and a comprehensive index help readers quickly locate particular subjects of interest. To guide students in further research, each volume features an extensive bibliography including books, periodicals, and related Internet websites. Finally, appendixes provide glossaries of terms, tables of measurements, chronological charts of major disasters, and related materials. With its many useful features, the Greenhaven Press Great Disasters series offers students a fascinating and awe-inspiring look at the deadly power of Earth's natural forces and their catastrophic impact on humans.

On August 23, 1992, residents of southeastern Florida rushed frantically to prepare for what appeared to be a moderately strong hurricane headed their way. While some people had gathered emergency supplies the day before, when a hurricane watch had been issued, many had put these tasks off until the watch was upgraded to a warning on the morning of the 23rd. Soon, supermarkets were stripped of food, batteries, and toilet paper, and lumber stores had run out of plywood for boarding up windows. On the following morning, Hurricane Andrew blasted in from the Atlantic Ocean and across south Florida. Dade County encountered sustained wind speeds of 145 miles per hour, with gusts up to 175 miles per hour. Although those in coastal regions had been evacuated, many regional inland residents had chosen to ride out the storm at home. Yet strong winds buffeted inland areas as well, and many people spent hours huddling in interior hallways and closets as the roofs and walls of their homes were torn away. After crossing south Florida, Andrew continued westward into the Gulf of Mexico and eventually turned north, hitting the central Louisiana coast on August 26.

Andrew was the third strongest—and the most economically devastating—hurricane to hit the mainland United States, with 25,524 homes destroyed and more than 100,000 others damaged. In Homestead, Florida, where the hurricane made its first landfall, 99 percent of mobile homes were destroyed. By the time Andrew hit southeastern Louisiana, it had weakened considerably, but it still spawned a powerful tornado that killed eight people. Overall, at least 300,000 people were left homeless, and total damages were tallied at more than $30 billion. Amazingly, however, the storm's death toll was relatively low, with twenty-three deaths in the United States and three deaths in the Bahamas. While some experts claim that good hurricane preparedness and evacuation plans helped to minimize the loss of life, others believe that the low death toll was a remarkably fortunate anomaly.

Those living in Central America in the fall of 1998 were not so lucky. On October 29, 1998, the deadliest hurricane to strike the Western Hemisphere in over two hundred years made landfall near Trujillo, Honduras. For more than fifteen hours, Hurricane Mitch battered the eastern Central America coast with sustained winds of 180 miles per hour, two hundred miles-per-hour gusts, and a forty-four foot storm surge—a wind-driven rise in sea level. Mitch was a sluggish hurricane, drifting slowly into the mountainous interior of Honduras and crossing over into Guatemala on October 31. The storm produced enormous amounts of precipitation—an estimated one to two feet per day—causing devastating floods and mudslides throughout Honduras, Nicaragua, Guatemala, Belize, and El Salvador. Whole villages were swept away or buried as rivers of mud came rushing down the mountainsides. At least ten thousand people were killed, and more than 3 million were left homeless.

Mitch is infamous not only for its intensity and high death toll, but also for its devastating aftermath. Honduran president Carlos Flores Facusse claimed that the storm obliterated the country's infrastructure and destroyed fifty years of progress. Survivors faced cholera and dengue fever as well as shortages of food, medicine, and water. Much of the banana, corn, bean, and coffee crops were destroyed, resulting in an estimated $900

*In August 1992, Hurricane Andrew spawned a powerful tornado that left at least 300,000 people homeless.*

million loss. In the ensuing months, affected regions were plagued by extreme poverty, hunger, and disease. Some experts predicted that it would take fifteen to twenty years for Honduras and Nicaragua to rebuild.

Mitch was a category five storm, a classification reserved for the most powerful hurricanes. The Saffir-Simpson Hurricane Intensity Scale, which rates storms on a scale of one to five, defines category five hurricanes as "catastrophic," while strong category four storms, such as Andrew, are described as "extreme." (See Appendix 1.) Storms like Mitch and Andrew, however, are relatively uncommon. During the entire twentieth century, only two category five hurricanes struck the U.S. mainland. On average, one to three hurricanes approach the U.S. coast each year, and the majority of these are category three or less. Still, the growing population along the Gulf coast and eastern seaboard increases the threat that these storms pose to life and property. Moreover, poor nations in Central America and the Caribbean region are especially vulnerable to even moderate hurricanes because many people live in simply constructed homes that are not very resistant to winds or floodwaters.

The process that fuels such powerful storms in the Atlantic basin starts in Africa, usually in the mid-to-late summer months. Strong thunderstorms moving westward off of the African continent create a tropical wave, a zone of disturbed weather that may become more organized and intense as it moves across the Atlantic Ocean. If this tropical disturbance moves over warm sea waters, it often forms a stormy circular area of low barometric air pressure near the ocean surface. At this point, several elements might come into play that could further intensify the weather system. One such element is a relatively cool, low-pressure air mass that moves in above the tropical disturbance—an "upper low." This positioning of the upper low creates an unstable atmosphere that leads to the development of convection. Convection starts as warm, humid air rises, a process that favors the growth of large thunderheads. When warm moist air rises, it condenses into water drops and releases heat, which in turn warms up the surrounding air. Subsequently, this air also rises. Meanwhile, the low pressure area at sea level draws in more warm, humid air from just above the ocean's surface. This air starts to rise more quickly, creating updraft winds. At the same time, horizontal humid winds—seemingly attempting to "replace" the air that is rising—begin to spiral toward the center of the low-pressure system. The earth's rotation causes these sea-level winds to flow in a counterclockwise direction in the Northern Hemisphere. The storm has now become a tropical depression.

As more heat energy is liberated and updrafts increase inside the storm's vortex, the barometric pressure continues to drop and the inrushing winds increase. When wind speeds increase beyond thirty-nine miles per hour, the depression is upgraded to a tropical storm. If the winds reach seventy-four miles per hour, the tropical storm is officially classified as a hurricane. Between 50 and 70 percent of tropical storms intensify into hurricanes.

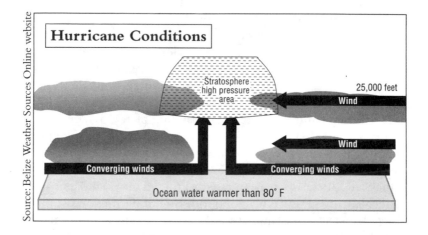

The size and strength of a hurricane is limited only by the humidity of the air, which is determined by ocean temperature. The warmer the seawater is, the more humid the surrounding air becomes, and the stronger the hurricane will be. Hurricanes can grow as large as six hundred miles in diameter, with wind speeds greater than two hundred miles per hour. Near the center of the storm, the effect of the earth's rotation prevents any further inward air movement. This inner boundary is the eye of the hurricane. The air around this central point spirals upward and then spreads out horizontally tens of thousands of feet above sea level. Seen from above, the hurricane appears as a mass of cirrostratus clouds diverging away from the eye.

When a hurricane hits a large land mass, it weakens relatively quickly because it no longer has warm ocean water to fuel it. Still, coastal communities hit by hurricanes are inundated with high winds, torrential rains, flooding, and occasional tornadoes. It may seem that powerful winds would pose the greatest threat to life and property; however, the sudden flooding resulting from the storm surge is actually a hurricane's most deadly element. The storm surge is a rapid rise in coastal sea level caused by massive, wind-driven waves. People who have taken shelter from the wind in strong, low-lying buildings may drown in a hurricane's storm surge. In the Galveston, Texas, hurricane of 1900, for example, most of the eight thousand deaths were drownings caused by the storm surge.

During the last half of the twentieth century, meteorologists and atmospheric scientists developed innovative technologies that enabled them to more accurately predict the intensity of hurricanes. Some ambitious researchers also experimented with methods of controlling hurricanes through cloud seeding. Yet today's weather experts are still not able to forecast precisely where a hurricane will hit more than two or three days ahead of time. This unattained goal—more exact landfall predictions—compels many scientists to pursue a deeper understanding of the dynamics of hurricanes, and they generally prefer to focus their efforts on improving the accuracy and lead time of forecasts rather than on controlling weather. This is probably for the best. As destructive as they are, hurricanes play an essential role in the earth's climate by rebalancing seasonal heat and moisture disparities across the planet. By all accounts, humans will have to coexist with this natural phenomenon. The best way to minimize the damage that hurricanes cause is to improve the science of weather forecasting.

# The Science and Study of Hurricanes

# The Nature of Hurricanes

## By David E. Fisher

*David E. Fisher is professor of cosmochemistry and director of the Environmental Science Program at the University of Miami. In the following selection Fisher describes how hurricanes form and some of the methods, instruments, and equations used to measure their intensity. He explains that hurricanes are fueled by a combination of warm, evaporating seawater, a low-pressure weather system, and an interplay between low-altitude and high-altitude winds. As warm, moist air flows into a low-pressure center, it rises, creating a partial vacuum—which in turn pulls in more warm winds. The lower the barometric pressure is at the center of a weather system, the greater the velocity of the inrushing winds, occasionally resulting in a hurricane. Fisher also discusses the most destructive element of a hurricane: the storm surge, which is a giant ocean wave generated by powerful winds.*

Hurricanes are basically gigantic heat pumps, gathering in the sun's energy over a region of hundreds of square miles and pumping it into the small center of the storm. The mechanism they use is evaporation of the warm tropical seawater, which transports the energy, and its subsequent condensation, which releases the heat into the interior. Like any engine, for it to keep running there has also to be a way to get rid of the exhaust: in this case, the dry air that results from the loss of water vapor. The mechanism for this is a high–altitude anticyclone, which sucks up the central dry air and spins it out hundreds of miles away. Air pressure is lowered in the center, where the warm, wet air is being sucked up to be spun away at high altitude, and with a low–pressure center, more air rushes in to fill the partial vacuum. Because of the earth's rotation and the storm

David E. Fisher, *The Scariest Place on Earth: Eye to Eye with Hurricanes.* New York: Random House, Inc., 1994. Copyright © 1994 by David E. Fisher. Reproduced by permission of the publisher.

center's position above (or below) the equator, the inrushing winds are spinning around the center as they try to move into it. The greater the difference in air pressure between the normal, outside air and the partial vacuum inside, the greater the velocity of these winds.

As the storm moves across the waters it can grow or weaken, depending largely on the coordination between inrushing surface winds and outpouring high-altitude winds. Since each of these is governed by separate steering currents—with wind direction and velocity changing drastically with altitude—it's very difficult to predict just what is going to happen from day to day. The hurricane can straggle along and never become much worse than a bad thunderstorm, or it can grow until it roars into a city with absolutely devastating force, killing more people and causing more damage than anything else in all of nature's arsenal. It can be more deadly than any earthquake or volcano, more devastating than any forest fire or mudslide. The hurricane that blasted Bangladesh in 1970 killed so many people that only rough estimates are possible, and these range up to 1 million dead, while Andrew [a 1992 South Florida hurricane] was to cause more damage in terms of material goods than any natural disaster in world history.

## Order Out of the Chaos

There is a world of difference between one hurricane and another. The storm that hit Miami [Florida] in 1966 did little more than rattle a few windows and dump a few inches of rain on the Everglades. The hurricane that hit Galveston, Texas, in 1900 killed nine thousand people.

To bring order out of this chaos Admiral Sir Francis Beaufort, hydrographer of the Royal Navy, proposed in 1806 a classification system for storms of all types. It was a simple numerical system running from zero to twelve, based on the force of the wind. Calm air, in which smoke rises vertically, was ranked as 0. When smoke began to drift, it was a 1; if you could feel the wind in your face, it became a 2. When leaves began to blow about, you had a force 3 wind; when dust and papers began to move around, you were in a force 4. Small trees sway in a force 5 breeze, and by the time it gets hard to keep an umbrella from blowing inside out, the wind is up to a 6. It becomes hard to walk against a force 7 wind, and an 8 begins to break branches off the trees. Bits of

roof come off in a 9, trees are uprooted by a 10, widespread damage accompanies an 11, and with a force 12 you have a hurricane:
"More or less complete destruction."

The original scale, as written above, was given in terms of typical observations a person might make rather than in terms of actual wind speed, because there was no way to measure wind speed
in 1806. Moreover, estimates of the strength of the wind became
more difficult to make in following years as steamships replaced
sailing vessels; in the latter you are moving more or less with the
wind and can feel its effects, while in the former sailors began to
move through the wind without respect to its force, and had to
estimate wind speeds by observing waves and spray. Not until
1846 was an accurate method of measuring the speed of the wind
invented, when J.T.R. Robinson, an Irish astronomer, presented
his anemometer. It was a simple instrument, consisting of four
hemispherical cups mounted on arms connected to a central rod.
The wind spun the cups, which spun the arms, which spun a dial,
which measured how fast the cups were rotating. With this advance it became possible to quantize the Beaufort scale, and we
now call a force 12 wind anything over seventy-five miles per
hour; that number becomes the defining criterion for a hurricane.

## Barometric Pressure

Wind speed is the most obvious thing one can measure in a hurricane, and accordingly it was the first. But what you really want
to know about a hurricane is a bit more than that. Scientists
studying the storm want to know about its structure and development, and people in its path want to know how severe it will
be. We can get a handle on both these questions if we know how
far the pressure at the center is dropping, because it is the difference in air pressure between the center and the surrounding areas that drives the winds. Air pressure, in fact, is the determining
factor in all weather prediction. It's a concept that was recognized
only relatively recently, although the instrument that measures it
was invented in 1643.

In that year an Italian named Evangelista Torricelli conceived
the idea that an empty room is not empty. Although the true nature of air was not demonstrated until 1783, . . . 141 years earlier
Torricelli was convinced that the nothing all around us must con-
sist of something. His reasoning is not known, but we can make
a guess at the kind of observations that stimulated him. Consider

a flame, for example. Put a glass over a lit candle and the flame will soon die out, suggesting that there must be something in the air that feeds it. Since this is demonstrably so, the "air" must be something, cannot be nothing.

Interesting idea. Others must have had similar thoughts, but what set Torricelli apart was that he devised a way to prove it. His idea was simplicity itself. Consider a hollow tube bent into a U shape and filled with liquid [see Figure 1].

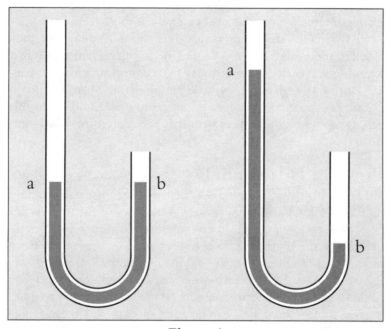

**Figure 1**

The liquid will obviously be at the same level in *a* and *b*. Even though this was intuitively obvious to everyone before him, it was Torricelli who suggested that it was due to the identical weight of the air above the liquid in the two places. Sealing off the tube on the left side *(a)* and pumping away the air above the liquid will leave no air to push down on *a*, and so the weight of air above *b* will force the liquid down.

And that is exactly what happened when Torricelli constructed his "barometer." Under normal atmospheric conditions the level of mercury at *a* will be seventy-six centimeters higher than at *b*. (Mercury is used because it is a liquid metal and thus has a low vapor pressure; that is, few atoms break away from its surface and fly around in a gaseous state. If a normal liquid such as water were used, the space above *a* would fill with a significant vapor pressure, which would then push down on the *a* column and disturb the reading.) If we imagine a column of air above the open inlet at *b*, there is a certain number of molecules in that column, each weighing a small but finite amount. At sea level the air in a column above a one-square-inch opening weighs 14.7 pounds, enough to push the liquid down seventy-six centimeters below the level at *a*, where there is no air.

In Torricelli's day this was not so obvious, since no one believed in molecules or atoms despite the fact that Democritus had hypothesized their existence more than two thousand years earlier. But by 1842 James Espy was arguing that the barometer was measuring the varying weight of the atmosphere, and it was this variation in weight (or pressure) that accounted for winds and storms. . . .

## Pressure Differentials

We know now that as air masses circulate over the earth building up areas of high and low pressure, molecules of air will stream from high to low pressure just as water will squirt from a nozzle because of the high pressure behind it and low pressure in front of it. This perpetual motion—fueled by the sun's uneven heating of the surface of the earth—provides not only our winds but all our weather. (The term "pressure" is used rather than "weight" because molecules of air are in constant motion, and as each molecule collides with something—which it does about 10 billion times a second—it exerts a pressure on it. Since this motion is random, pressure is exerted in all directions, unlike weight, which simply exerts pressure "down." It is this omnidirectional pressure that keeps us from feeling the weight of the atmosphere: the molecules inside our body are pushing out with the same force that the air molecules are pushing in; the air molecules under an extended hand are pushing up with as much force as those above it are pushing down.)

The winds of a hurricane are no exception to these laws, and are related to the difference in pressure between the center of the storm and the outside world by a simple equation:

$$Wind\ Velocity = 6.3\sqrt{Pressure\ Difference}$$

The pressure differential is related to the ocean surface temperature, and since the wind velocity is related to the wind energy and thus its potential for destruction, the damage a hurricane does is directly proportional to the pressure difference inside and outside of the eye. It's intuitively obvious that the more energy a wind has, the more damage it can do; and you probably remember from high school that $E = \frac{1}{2}(mass) \times (velocity)^2$. Nor should the relation between ocean temperature and pressure difference come as a surprise: since the hurricane is driven by the solar-heat engine (the sun heating the ocean waters, which then evaporate and feed the storm), it should be intuitively obvious that the warmer the ocean temperatures the more energy is available for the hurricane, which means the faster the central air column will rise, creating even lower pressure there. . . .

## Wind and Temperature

Robert Merrill, who in 1985 showed that a high-altitude anticyclone over the low-altitude cyclone was a necessary part of starting a hurricane, also provided an estimate of the maximum potential wind speed as a function of seawater temperature.

The graph (Figure 2) makes clear that in order to get a hurricane going, seawater temperatures greater than about 25 degrees Centigrade are needed, and the ferocity of a hurricane can rise steeply as the ocean waters get warmer degree by degree. This great variation in the intensity of hurricanes gives rise to a need for hurricane classification; that is, for an extension of the Beaufort scale into the hurricane region. This need was met in 1975 by two meteorologists, Herbert Saffir and Robert Simpson, and their Hurricane Damage Scale is now widely used.

(The unit of pressure used in the scale is the millibar, rather than pounds/square inch. The millibar is one thousandth of a bar, which is the force exerted by 100,000 Newtons over an area of one square meter, where a Newton is the force needed to accelerate a—never mind. The millibar has become the popular unit of measurement because normal atmospheric pressure is nearly one thousand millibars [actually 1013.25 millibars], and so the degree of deviation from this is clearly visualized. My textbook tells me that when we convert to the metric system—"probably early in the 1990s"—this unit will be replaced by the Pascal. Ha!)

The Sunday [Miami] *Herald* reported Andrew's winds reaching 110 miles per hour as it approached Miami, making it "al-

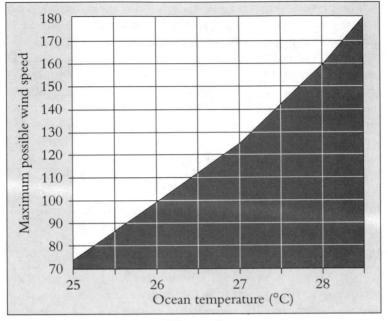

**Figure 2**

most a Category 3 hurricane." That indicates a storm surge of nine to twelve feet, which scared the hell out of me when my father asked if he couldn't stay in his high-rise condo a couple of hundred yards from the Atlantic Ocean.

Hell, no, I said.

## The Storm Surge

When most people think of hurricanes they think of winds, and it's true that most economic damage is done by the hundred-mile-an-hour-and-up winds, but it's the storm surge that kills people. By the thousands. By the hundreds of thousands.

Take a quick look at the left part of Figure 1. The liquid level is at the same height in *a* and *b*. Now imagine that these two spots represent different places in the world ocean. (The U-shaped tube need not be there; it serves only to connect the water at *a* and *b*.) Under normal conditions they assume the same height, but should the air pressure over *a* be reduced while that at *b* stays the same, this will obviously create a rise in water level at *a* (as in the right part of Figure 1).

What could reduce the air pressure over *a*? A hurricane, of course, which begins with a concentrated area of low pressure rising off the ocean surface. (The winds pour into this low-pressure area, it is true, but never bring the pressure back up to normal; if they do, the hurricane is over.) The low air pressure over the growing center of the hurricane acts on the water beneath it just as the evacuated space above *a* does in Figure 1: as the pressure drops, the level of the liquid rises. The most powerful hurricanes have the lowest central pressures—below 920 millibars, according to the Saffir-Simpson scale—and the ocean water at the center can rise more than eighteen feet above normal.

And there are other factors to aggravate the situation. The storm surge is, after all, a sort of combination giant wave and supertide, and so all the factors that normally affect and create winds and tides can do so here as well. All waves are generated by winds blowing over the ocean surface, and the height of the wave depends on how much energy the wind transfers to the water by frictional interaction. The energy transfer depends on three things: the wind speed, the length of time it blows, and the distance that the wind travels over open water. In a hurricane the wind speed is obviously great, but so too are the other two factors, and the resulting waves are much larger than they would be if the hurricane suddenly sprang into existence a short distance offshore.

## Hurricane Waves

Another factor affecting the final storm surge is the depth of the ocean floor, which decreases steeply as the storm approaches the continent. This is important because of the behavior of all waves. In deep water the movement of the wave is quite different from that of the water within it. The wave is moving forward, but the water mass is not. A piece of wood floating on the ocean surface remains where it is as successive waves move along beneath it: the wood bobs up and down, marking the movement of the water molecules that surround it: the water molecules move vertically up and down as the wave passes, but they don't move along with it.

This vertical motion diminishes with increased depth beneath the wave. But now what happens when the wave approaches shore and the ocean floor begins to rise toward the continent? When the depth is shallow enough the vertically bobbing water hits bottom, which happens when the depth shortens to about half the wavelength, the distance between successive wave crests. Some of the wave energy is then spent as frictional loss against the ocean bottom—just as the wind transferred energy to the water, now the water transfers energy to the sandy bottom. Other than moving some bottom particles around, this process also causes the wave to lose energy and slow down. And this means that the wave behind it catches up, and merges with it. The resulting wave grows higher and pushes its vertical motion down more forcefully, thereby losing more energy to the ocean floor and slowing further so that succeeding waves catch up and pile into a higher wave. Eventually the total weight of water above sea level is too great to be supported and the wave turns over and crashes down, creating a surf.

This is the normal wave pattern, magnified of course by the increased energy of a hurricane. Normal surf is influenced greatly by the topography of the ocean bottom near the shore—how steeply it rises—and by the distance of open water at great depth over which the waves have traveled. This is why some beaches—at Atlantic City, [New Jersey] or Ogunquit, Maine—have wonderful surf, while others have little or none. (The greatest disappointment of my life, after realizing at the age of eight or nine that I would never really be able to fly like Superman, was when we moved to Miami, and I raced out to the beach with my surfboard and then stood dumbfounded, watching the ocean just sitting there, barely moving. This is because of the Bahamas Bank, which sits offshore and intercepts the ocean waves; the distance between the Bank and the Miami beaches isn't great enough to allow a decent surf to grow, except under exceptionally strong winds.)

Normally, surf is a wonderful thing. But when a hurricane strikes, the combination of excessive wind speed and the long time duration of the storm and the large distance it has traveled means that the waves can rise to a great height before they come crashing down. This effect is magnified with disastrous consequences if the storm hits land at a time of normal high tide. It's a fearsome spectacle to imagine, even more terrible to actually see. When all three factors combine, hurricane waves greater than thirty-feet high can come crashing ashore. Imagine a wall of water as high as a four-story building rushing at you with all the force of a hurricane. For hundreds of thousands of people, this was the last thing they saw on this earth: on average, 90 percent of the loss of life in a hurricane is due to the storm surge washing ashore and flooding the coastal area under a moving mountain of water. The storm surge is the most deadly force in all of nature.

## The Bangladesh Disaster

The Pacific is the largest ocean, with, obviously, the greatest chance of waves moving over the greatest distance before hitting shore, and here is indeed where the worst storm surges have hit. The giant tidal waves formed by hurricanes or suboceanic earthquakes, the tsunamis, are part of Japanese lore. But it was on the subcontinent of India that one of the worst disasters in the history of the world occurred.

It happened in Bangladesh, in what was then East Pakistan, on November 13, 1970. Those familiar with the signs knew a storm was brewing in the Bay of Bengal; those who could not read the signs knew nothing, for there was no warning service to speak of. An American weather satellite had spotted a low-pressure area being blown into the bay from the direction of Malay, and had duly notified the Pakistani government. The Pakistani weather bureau followed the storm as it intensified and moved northwest toward the Ganges delta, where a series of densely occupied islands, barely a few feet above sea level, stood waiting for it. The government had built dikes that circled some of these islands, and they were to prove . . . [ineffectual] in stopping the waters. . . . The government tried to warn the people what was coming, but there was no effective communication service—no televisions, few radios, and even fewer telephones.

It didn't really matter. Knowing the storm was coming could not have averted it, and there was no way for the people to evacuate: no highways, no cars, no airplanes. Some of the people heard the radio broadcasts and knew that a bad storm was on its way: they boarded up their windows. What else could they do?

Useless, totally useless. About midnight the people on the islands farthest from shore heard a rumbling sound that grew slowly at first but turned quickly into a frightening roar. Peering out their windows they saw a luminous cloud in the darkness, sitting low on the water. As they watched, the cloud came closer, growing in height and roaring until the ground shook and the flimsy wooden houses trembled, and then it rose up out of the waters and they saw that the glittering whiteness was the crest of a wave which towered over them and then came crashing down—and that was the last sight they ever saw.

> And what rough beast, its hour come round at last,
> Slouches toward Bethlehem to be born?

Later, six children remembered their grandfather gathering them up and throwing them into a wooden crate. Three days passed before the crate was seen bobbing up and down in the ocean, and the children were rescued. But they never saw their grandfather, or any of their family, again.

Reporters who flew over the islands in the days following saw corpses floating in the paddies, corpses littering the beaches, the bodies of men and women mixed with dead cattle and horses. Too many to count, too many to bury. Estimates run close to 1 million people dead, although to this day no one knows how many for sure. "What can we do?" the president of Pakistan explained. "We can only pray to Allah for mercy."

Right. Lots of luck.

# Predicting the Intensity of Hurricanes

## By Robert Henson

*In the following selection Robert Henson discusses the challenges that meteorologists face in forecasting the intensity of hurricanes. Hurricanes are often elusive, strengthening and weakening in unpredictable ways. A lack of vital data about upper-level winds and deep-water temperatures in the tropics has hindered scientists' efforts to forecast when and if a hurricane will strengthen, Henson points out. Recently, however, new computer models and observational technologies have begun to help researchers sort out the complex factors contributing to a hurricane's intensity. Henson is a writer and editor at the University Corporation for Atmospheric Research in Boulder, Colorado. He is also a contributing editor of* Weatherwise, *a monthly periodical.*

How strong will a hurricane get? The question remains tantalizing, but new data are yielding fresh clues. Year by year, we've narrowed down the forecast tracks of tropical cyclones.

Hurricane death tolls in the United States are now in the dozens instead of the hundreds or even thousands. Some forecasters claim to be able to estimate months in advance how many tropical cyclones the Atlantic and Gulf of Mexico might spawn in a given season.

Our nation's hurricane specialists have much to be proud of. You might think things are in hand by now, as if every aspect of hurricane prediction is on a smooth course toward earlier and better warnings. True in part.

But then, we run into "the intensity problem." Any forecaster who's dealt with storms like 1995's Hurricane Opal will attest to the difficulty in predicting when and how much a tropical cyclone will strengthen or weaken. Meteorologists typically inch forward, chipping away at a problem with faster computers or better instruments, but the intensity problem refuses to budge.

Even while NOAA's [the National Oceanic and Atmospheric Administration's] National Hurricane Center (NHC) forecasts of tracks and landfall locations have improved, forecasts of hurricane strength have shown virtually no improvement. . . . Progress is being made in certain areas, but the big picture still eludes researchers. And the storms that change the fastest pose the biggest challenges.

## Opal and the Intensity Problem

[In 1995], Hurricane Opal provided a chilling illustration of how the intensity problem casts a shadow over our present-day warning system. At 10 A.M. on Tuesday, October 3, Opal was drifting northward into the central Gulf of Mexico. At that point, it was a Category 1 on the Saffir-Simpson scale, with top winds of 90 m.p.h. The official forecast brought Opal into the Pensacola, Florida, vicinity Wednesday evening as a Category 2.

But Opal had other ideas. Overnight, the storm's barometric pressure plummeted from 965 to 916 millibars and its peak sustained winds jumped to 150 m.p.h., making Opal a strong Category 4. Even worse, Opal's forward motion almost tripled, exceeding 20 m.p.h. That meant the storm would come ashore Wednesday afternoon, cutting critical hours from the window of evacuation time. "Not only was Opal intensifying, but it was accelerating. Those are two things you don't want to go together," says Mark DeMaria, a NHC technical specialist and backup forecaster who was on hand the night Opal suddenly raged.

The late notice and evacuation delays could have meant catastrophic damage to the Gulf Coast, except for yet another unexpected change in intensity—this one a drop from strong Category 4 to weak Category 3 status in the final hours before Opal's 5 P.M. landfall. As it was, Opal was bad enough. The storm caused some $3 billion in damage, several storm-related deaths, and countless numbers of frayed nerves.

Scientists are finding the intensity problem too important—and too intriguing—to be ignored. A few years ago, the American Meteorological Society held a panel discussion under the wistful header, "Is There Any Hope for Tropical Cyclone Intensity Prediction?"

More recently, a two-day symposium at the society's 1998 annual meeting focused debate on the many factors that make forecasting hurricane strength so difficult. These problems are rooted in both observation and theory. Vast gaps in oceanic and atmospheric data across the tropics make it hard to tell if a hurricane has the right stuff to strengthen.

But even when the prerequisites are clearly present, many tropical cyclones fail to meet their potential, like so many underachieving students. And it's the "rapid intensifiers"—those rare storms such as Opal that go through a few hours of serious sustained strengthening to take them from minor to major hurricane status—that present the greatest challenge to forecasters.

## Revving Up the Engine

The basics that drive hurricane behavior aren't mysterious. At heart, a tropical cyclone is a heat engine. As a tropical wave evolves into a depression, which can in turn become a tropical storm and then a hurricane, the system pulls ocean-warmed, 80°F air inward and upward. It flays that warm, moist air back outward eight to twelve miles above sea level, where temperatures can be as cold as −100°F. The energy extracted as the air expands and cools in updrafts around the eye is translated into the kinetic energy of a hurricane's violent winds.

Simple and powerful as it is, the hurricane heat engine can sputter at any number of places—including ignition. Showers and thunderstorms might focus on one side of a tropical wave or depression, precluding the formation of a symmetric eye. The system might pass over cool waters that tend to inhibit convection. Strong upper-level winds might tilt the circulation, causing it to weaken. Or the system could run into a mountainous island that disrupts the low-level flow.

This is why dozens of waves parade westward across the tropical Atlantic in any given season, yet only a handful develop into systems strong enough to earn themselves names. The best that forecasters can do is declare when conditions are generally favorable for a given storm to intensify, then keep a close eye on it.

Warm sea-surface temperatures (SSTs) are a must. Upper-level winds that diverge, or that blow in sync with the low-level cir-

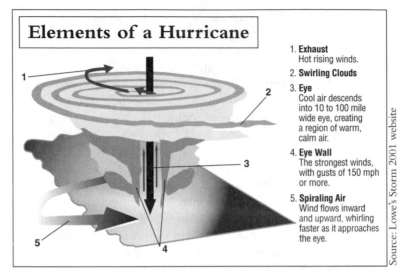

**Elements of a Hurricane**

1. **Exhaust**
   Hot rising winds.
2. **Swirling Clouds**
3. **Eye**
   Cool air descends
   into 10 to 100 mile
   wide eye, creating
   a region of warm,
   calm air.
4. **Eye Wall**
   The strongest winds,
   with gusts of 150 mph
   or more.
5. **Spiraling Air**
   Wind flows inward
   and upward, whirling
   faster as it approaches
   the eye.

Source: Lowe's Storm 2001 website

culation, allow for a stronger updraft. Climatology points to certain areas at certain times of year—for instance, the Cape Verde region off western Africa in August and September. Yet even when all these factors are favorable, many systems refuse to grow in the way a forecaster might expect.

"You never know which waves are going to develop," says Lixion Avila, a hurricane specialist at NHC. If a wave starts to grow, and the environment looks nurturing, then the NHC usually extrapolates its growth in a straight-line fashion. "If there's an upward trend, we tend to catch it," says Avila. "Generally we're on the right track, but it's a very complicated process. There are many things that we can't observe and we don't understand."

Upper-level wind data, for instance, is especially sparse in the tropics, which complicates forecasts of motion as well as intensity. Satellites and buoys keep regular tabs on SSTs, but not on the deeper water that now seems important for the strongest hurricanes. And there is usually little surface data over the open seas to indicate whether a closed low-pressure center has formed and, if so, how strong it is.

NHC's typical intensity error is about 12 m.p.h. at 24 hours and around 18 m.p.h. (roughly one Saffir-Simpson category) by 48 hours. Rapid intensifiers are especially hard to catch in advance. [In 1997] in the eastern Pacific, the first 72-hour intensity forecast for new Tropical Storm Linda put it at 60 knots (70 m.p.h.), which would have kept Linda just below hurricane strength. Linda's actual strength 72 hours later turned out to be an incredible 160 knots (185 m.p.h.).

# Number Crunching Still Comes Up Short

While a number of models are skillful at showing where mature storms will track, those same models might eagerly develop too many waves into hurricanes. Only one model is tailor-made for predicting intensity. It takes its cues from the climatological record of hundreds of tropical cyclones and then blends those statistics with current conditions and the recent trend of the storm at hand (strengthening, weakening, or steady-state). In the past several years, the NHC has also begun using intensity outlooks from its premier track model created at NOAA's Geophysical Fluid Dynamics Laboratory and thus dubbed the GFDL model.

"The GFDL model is starting to show skill in forecasting intensity beyond 48 hours," says modeling expert Sim Aberson from NOAA's Atlantic Oceanographic and Meteorological Laboratory (AOML). "That's the pattern we first saw with track models in the 1970s. I think it's a problem we're finally getting a grasp on."

# Strength Testing

Since the 1960s, satellites have been a mainstay for tracking tropical cyclones and estimating their intensity. Researcher Vernon Dvorak created a system in the 1970s that is still the most widely used tool worldwide for analyzing tropical-cyclone intensity and position. The Dvorak technique correlates peak winds with familiar satellite signatures, such as the anticyclonic swirl of cirrus that surrounds major storms. But the system is subjective: it depends on the skilled eye of the forecaster to interpret the satellite image.

Another tool for measuring intensity is hurricane-hunter aircraft. The planes are often sent into even weak waves if the conditions appear right for growth. By collecting observations in flight, and depositing "dropsondes" that send back reports as they fall through the storm, the planes gather far more detailed data than standard observations can provide.

New developments in hurricane hunting have provided some long-awaited hints toward improvement in intensity outlooks. A high-flying Gulfstream jet now allows more thorough sampling of the upper-level outflow that indicates a hurricane's health and the steering winds that guide its motion. In five flights during the 1997 season, the Gulfstream sampled the Atlantic's Erika and Claudette and the Pacific's Linda. When fed into the GFDL model, the Gulfstream's upper-air data produced up to a 32 percent improvement in track forecasts and a 20 percent improvement in the model's intensity forecasts out to 48 hours.

The Gulfstream, along with other hurricane-hunting aircraft such as the veteran P-3, are also making use of new dropsondes developed by the National Center for Atmospheric Research (NCAR), based on Global Positioning System (GPS) technology, the new dropsondes gather a picture of the hurricane's inner eyewall unavailable with its predecessor, the Omega sonde. Humidity sensors on the old sondes would get wet inside a cloud and report 100 percent humidity from that point on—even after falling below cloud base.

The new sondes can obtain accurate humidity readings in the all-important air that feeds into updrafts from below cloud level. Aircraft data also help tell how moist the upper atmosphere is. The tropics actually tend to be relatively dry more than two or three miles above the surface, where relative humidities average around 50 percent. Hurricanes prefer to form within "moist towers," scattered deep clumps of more humid air that can insulate a developing storm.

Winds in the atmosphere around the storm are also critical. If lower-level speed and direction differs too much from upper levels, the vertical hurricane engine gets pulled apart over time. The older sonde computed an average wind every 1,600 feet along its vertical path, so the final wind report was usually several hundred feet above sea level—not a true surface wind. The GPS sonde reports back every 16 feet, so forecasters now have the best readings to date of low-level storm winds and their distribution around the eye.

Data on eyewall behavior is especially valuable. The eyes of rapid intensifiers usually contract, which helps their spin to increase (just as a spinning figure skater speeds up when he pulls in his arms). In time, a new eyewall may form around the first one as the latter collapses on itself. This cycle may take as little as 12 hours or as long as two days—and precious little is known about why or how it happens. "Nobody can tell you that in 48 hours there's going to be an eyewall cycle taking place," notes Avila.

# Underneath It All

Warm seas represent the fuel for hurricane growth. One of the most important numbers in hurricane intensity is 26°C, or 79°F—the minimum SST needed for a hurricane to thrive (give or take a degree depending on the situation). It's largely the release of oceanic heat into the air through evaporation that fuels the storm. The stronger the winds and the warmer the SSTs, the greater the evaporation rate. This positive feedback helps a well-structured storm to grow explosively when nothing outside the hurricane interferes. But strong surface winds also produce chaotic seas, and the water churned up from below may be far cooler than the sun-warmed surface temperatures detected from satellites.

Like oil and vinegar in a bottle, the ocean is arranged into at least two distinct layers: a warm surface pool, or mixed layer and colder deep water. The boundary in between, called the thermocline, usually rests from 100 to 150 feel below the surface across the tropical Atlantic. This can be shallow enough for the wind and wave-driven turbulence of a hurricane to bring cold water up into the mixed layer, a negative feedback that bodes ill for the storms' intensity.

But there are places where the thermocline may dip much lower, to 300 or 350 feet, across a zone one or two hundred miles wide. In such places—as in the Gulf Stream that hugs the Atlantic coast, or in warm-core eddies that move westward across the Gulf of Mexico—a hurricane may do its worst and still have a reservoir of deep warm water from which to draw sustained energy. (For instance, Hurricane Andrew reached peak intensity as it passed over the Gulf Stream just before striking south Florida in August 1992.)

It's becoming clear that SSTs alone aren't enough to determine how hurricane-supportive a patch of ocean is. "The first meter of SST in front of a storm is eroded away in minutes to hours. You've got to think about the deeper mixed layer and the depth of the thermocline," says Lynn "Nick" Shay, an oceanographer at the University of Miami. What's needed is three-dimensional ocean data. Shay and NOAA/AOML Oceanographer Gustavo Goni are developing a satellite-based technique to provide just that.

Because water expands as it warms, the sea surface above a warm-core eddy may form a dome up to a foot higher than the surrounding sea level. A radar-based altimeter aboard NASA's TOPEX/Poseidon satellite mission can produce a precise measure of the height of the sea surface. It actually measures these domes. By combining that data with a climatology of deepwater conditions, researchers can estimate the depth of water that's warmer than 80°F.

## The Mystery at the Heart of Hurricanes

[In 1998] the new data will be tested in forecast mode for the first time at NHC for the Gulf of Mexico. In research mode, the deepwater measurements have already shed light on Hurricane Opal, a favorite case study for intensity research because of the classic yet complex atmospheric and oceanic factors involved.

There were two main contributors to Opal's frenzied intensification and its dramatic weakening. One was a large upper-level trough that was approaching the Gulf from Texas. Although big troughs tend to produce too much shear for hurricanes, they can also shed smaller pieces of circulation that enhance hurricanes' spin, which may have helped to strengthen Opal.

The other contributor was a warm-core eddy pinched off from the Loop Current that circumscribes the Caribbean. This eddy drifted westward at a few miles per day after leaving the Loop Current, winding up in the central Gulf as Opal approached. According to a set of model simulations performed at the Naval Research Laboratory by Simon Chang and graduate student Xiadong Hong, up to 60 percent of Opal's rapid intensification can be ascribed to the warm-core eddy. Opal's later weakening coincided with its passage from the warm eddy to shallower, slightly cooler waters near the Gulf Coast, along with the approach of the main upper-level trough.

For all these promising leads on Opal, and on its fellow rapid intensifiers, mystery still lies at the heart of hurricanes' ups and downs "It's like a chess game. You have so many factors going on at the same time," says Avila.

Even the intensity of past hurricanes is under scrutiny. The AOML's Chris Landsea is leading a three-year NOAA project to examine over a century of hurricanes using modern analysis techniques. As technology has evolved, so have the ways of estimating peak surface winds of hurricanes—from estimates based on damage to satellite-based estimates, from calculations based on dropsonde-derived central pressure to today's precise GPS-based wind data. The new project will apply a uniform yardstick to these measurements.

For instance, says Landsea, "We know that in the 1940s through the 1960s, winds were being overestimated based on central pressure." Could this project result in some famous old storms losing or gaining in their Saffir-Simpson ranking? "It's a certainty," says Landsea.

What remains uncertain is the future of hurricane intensity prediction. The latest models and satellite-based observational tools provide some optimism. "The new dropsondes are incredible data collectors, even in the midst of hurricane-force winds," says Landsea. However, there is still tough science ahead in figuring out what makes some hurricanes turn nasty so quickly. According to AOML's Sim Aberson, "The big problem is the rapid intensifiers like Opal. I think they'll remain a major problem for many years to come."

# Hurricanes and Global Warming

BY DAVID BJERKLIE AND DICK THOMPSON

*Higher ocean temperatures spurred by global warming may lead to an increase in catastrophic hurricanes, report* Time *writers David Bjerklie and Dick Thompson in the following selection. Warm sea water generally provides a good breeding ground for powerful hurricanes. However, other factors, such as wind and ocean currents, West African rainfall amounts, and varying El Niño and La Niña conditions also determine the development of hurricanes. For example, El Niño—a warming of Pacific waters—actually inhibits Atlantic hurricanes because it creates westerly winds that impede the buildup of storm clouds with hurricane potential. Moreover, initially strong hurricanes spawned by warmer oceans could actually stir up deeper cooler waters, causing them to weaken and die.*

Human memories are short, and even as the tattered ghost of Hurricane Floyd finally blew itself out over eastern Canada [in September 1999], it was easy to forget that it began the week as a meteorological giant—one of the [twentieth] century's largest and most powerful Atlantic storms. If it seems as if hurricanes are getting stronger these days, that's because they are. After a 30-year lull, the U.S. is once again being visited by hurricanes the size of the ones that battered the Eastern seaboard in the 1940s, '50s and '60s. Thanks to an unlucky confluence of events—warm Atlantic waters, brisk trade winds and some strange doings in the eastern Pacific—we're on the cusp of what could be an extended spell of very heavy weather.

Floyd is nothing, scientists warn, compared with what may lie ahead. In the [twenty-first] century, they say, we may see hurricanes that far exceed Floyd's top sustained winds and approach a

David Bjerklie and Dick Thompson, "Wait Till Next Time: If a Little Heated Water in the Atlantic Can Create Floyd, What Storms Will Global Warming Bring?" *Time*, vol. 154, September 27, 1999, p. 38. Copyright © 1999 by Time, Inc. Reproduced by permission.

hurricane's upper limit of 180 m.p.h.—more than capable of sending a 30-ft. wall of water surging inland, flattening houses, inundating coastal cities and stirring the ocean bottom to a depth of 600 ft.

Moreover, that 180-m.p.h. speed limit pertains only to present conditions. There's now a wild card in the climatic deck, observes M.I.T. [Massachusetts Institute of Technology] atmospheric scientist Kerry Emanuel: global warming. Over coming decades, atmospheric pollution and the greenhouse effect are expected to heat not just the air but also the surface of the oceans, and it is the thermal energy of that water that fuels typhoons and hurricanes. As a rule of thumb, according to Emanuel, wind speeds increase 5 m.p.h. for every additional degree Fahrenheit of water temperature. By that formula, sustained winds in future hurricanes could conceivably top 200 m.p.h.

But even these storms, it should be noted, would look puny compared with the megastorm of unimaginable destructiveness that scientists have dubbed a "hypercane." Indeed, some meteorologists speculate that a runaway hypercane, triggered by the splashdown of a giant asteroid, may have been instrumental in wiping out the dinosaurs 65 million years ago.

What makes hurricanes? They are, in essence, just big wind machines that move heat from the equator to the poles. While they do this very efficiently, the same task could be performed by swarms of independent thunderstorms. It takes a certain amount of magic, in other words, to set a hurricane in motion. First, you have to make the thunderstorms, and then "you have to get the thunderstorms dancing," as Florida State University climatologist James O'Brien puts it. "You have to get them dancing in a big circle dance."

In Floyd's case, the dance started when a disturbance high in the atmosphere moved off the coast of Africa and out over the Atlantic. Fueled by the rise of warm, humid air (in places, sea surface temperatures measured a steamy 86°F), the disturbance very quickly spawned a brood of thunderstorms that coalesced in a slow-moving whorl known as a tropical depression. On September 8, as its winds reached 40 m.p.h., Floyd became a tropical storm. On September 10, when its winds topped 74 m.p.h., it became a Category 1 hurricane. A few days later, with winds approaching 155 m.p.h., Floyd very nearly became a Category 5 storm—the highest category of all.

Meteorologists all agree that the energy powering Floyd—
making it bigger than the average hurricane—came from the
warmth of the water below. The tropical North Atlantic . . . was
unusually warm [that fall] as it was during the period of high
hurricane activity from the 1940s to the 1960s. Then, between
about 1979 and 1995, the tropical North Atlantic cooled, and
hurricane activity slackened. Now, notes David Enfield, a researcher at the Atlantic Oceanographic and Meteorological Laboratory in Miami, temperatures in this sector of ocean appear to
be trending up once more. Like other oceanographers, Enfield
believes this is the result of a natural climate shift, as opposed to
human-induced global warming.

While warm water may be essential to the making of a hurricane, it is not sufficient. Colorado State University meteorologist William Gray points out. Gray has pioneered a hurricane-
forecasting system that folds in many factors, including the
strength of stratospheric winds, large-scale changes in ocean circulation, the amount of rainfall in West Africa and swings between El Nino and La Nina conditions in the equatorial Pacific.
Indeed, says Gray, one reason the 1999 hurricane season [was] so
active [was] that [a] La Nina [had] persisted for more than a year.

Why would El Nino (which warms Pacific waters) and La
Nina (which cools them) affect hurricanes in an entirely different ocean? The explanation is simple. El Nino enhances the influence of high-level westerly winds that swoop across the Atlantic, decapitating developing storm clouds before hurricanes
can spawn. La Nina, by contrast, favors a more easterly flow that
allows these clouds to mature into towering turrets, gathering energy as they grow. Florida State's O'Brien and two of his students
have recently established that the chance of two or more hurricanes hitting the Eastern U.S. stands at about 25% when El Nino
is ascendant but jumps to 75% when La Nina reigns.

Because of the El Nino and La Nina effects, and all those
other factors, figuring out what might happen to hurricanes in a
warmer world is, well, complicated. "Anything that does happen
will likely cause only small changes," says Gray. "And no one can
say which way these changes will go." If global warming favors
more El Nino and fewer La Nina events, for instance, then the
distribution of hurricanes will undoubtedly shift. But while there
will be more typhoons in the Pacific and fewer hurricanes in the
Atlantic, the total number of major storms is likely to remain the

same. Worldwide, scientists think, there will probably continue to be about 80 such events in any given year.

How strong will those storms be? That's harder to estimate, in part because a very big storm is in some ways its own worst enemy. "A hurricane has a noticeable cooling effect on the ocean," explains atmospheric scientist Kevin Trenberth of the National Center for Atmospheric Research (NCAR). Indeed, at a certain stage of its life cycle, a storm of a given size will stir up enough cold water to put a halt to its growth. At that point, scientists say, it has come into equilibrium. Maintaining that balance is especially hard, because if a hurricane stirs up too much cold water, it will weaken and die. This suicidal tendency no doubt helps account for the fact that Category 5 hurricanes are so rare. Indeed, only two . . . hit the U.S. during [the twentieth] century, among them the 1969 hurricane named Camille.

How was it that Camille managed to grow so powerful? One reason, says Emanuel, is the path that Camille chose. She (in those days all hurricanes were of the feminine persuasion) faithfully followed the meanderings of the "loop current," a tributary of the Gulf Stream. It wasn't that the loop current was any warmer than the surrounding water at the surface, notes Emanuel, but its warmth went much deeper. Result: Camille's winds stirred up warm water as opposed to cold, and thus retained their strength.

Suppose, for the sake of argument, that global warming does cause the intensity of hurricanes to increase to supercane proportions. How stable would such megastorms be? A hurricane packing 200-m.p.h. winds would be significantly more powerful than Camille, whose top sustained winds were in the 180-m.p.h. range. Such a supercane would be capable, certainly, of taking a catastrophic toll, but its winds would also presumably penetrate to greater depths. Long before making landfall, a supercane might stir up a lethal dose of chilly water. More intense storms, in other words, could prove to be exceedingly fragile entities.

Of course, there are other ways in which global warming might boost the power of hurricanes. It's possible, for instance, that in a warmer world hurricanes might tank up with a lot more rain, which would greatly increase the damage caused by flooding. In addition, storm surges could be expected to become a lot more lethal if, as many anticipate, global sea levels rise.

But as NCAR's Roger Pielke Jr. observes, it's really not necessary to concoct ways to make hurricanes any more threatening than they already are. With or without global warming, there are going to be some whoppers in our future, and unlike Floyd, many of these will prove to be megadisasters. For the days when a big hurricane could make landfall in sparsely populated places are fast disappearing, Pielke notes, and that alone is cause enough for worry.

# Hunting Prehistoric Hurricanes

## By John Tarvis

*Solid data on past U.S. hurricanes is available for only the past 150 years, which is not a large enough span of time for today's scientists to statistically estimate the frequency of major hurricanes. However, as science writer John Tarvis explains in the following selection, the new field of paleotempestology may assist investigators in such efforts. Paleotempestology—the study of prehistoric hurricanes—entails examining the sediment layers underneath coastal lakes and marshes for telltale signs of catastrophic storms. The storm surge of a hurricane forces ocean and beach sand inland, notes Tarvis, and this sand eventually settles at the bottom of regional lakes. Researchers document prehistoric hurricanes by taking core samples of lakebed sediment. Inspecting coral, tree rings, trapped pollen, and clam shells also offers clues about primeval cyclones.*

On September 9, 1900, the impossible destroyed Galveston, Texas. A fierce hurricane roared over the thriving coastal city that day, flooding its island with water and claiming more than 6,000 lives, about 1 in every 5 residents. The storm arrived with almost no warning. The U.S. Weather Bureau had ignored forecasts of Cuban meteorologists, noting that a severe hurricane had never before hit the town.

Judged simply on its strength, the hurricane that leveled Galveston a century ago was indeed a rare phenomenon. Meteorologists today classify it as a category 4 storm—one with sustained winds of 131 to 155 miles per hour. Few of those monsters ever arise in the Atlantic Ocean's hurricane breeding grounds, let alone smash into the U.S. mainland. In the past 150 years, fewer than a dozen have struck the U.S. coast along the Gulf of Mexico or the Atlantic.

The most catastrophic hurricanes, known as category 5, are even more uncommon. Just two have run into the United States in the past century. In 1935, on Labor Day, one flattened the Florida Keys. In 1969, Hurricane Camille roared through Mississippi.

The infrequency of severe hurricanes is welcome news, of course. Yet it also poses a problem. Reliable data on hurricane landfalls in the United States is available only for the past 150 years. And given the small number of category 4 and 5 storms during that relatively short time span, scientists don't have enough statistical power to estimate confidently how frequently catastrophic hurricanes strike the U.S. coastline.

So, to better look forward, investigators have decided to look further back in time. As part of a fledgling discipline called paleotempestology, they've begun to search for signs of hurricanes that predate recorded history.

At the forefront of this effort is Kam-biu Liu of Louisiana State University in Baton Rouge. By unearthing sand layers deposited by massive hurricanes in coastal lakes and marshes, his research group has identified storms that have struck the U.S. coast over the past 5,000 years. In February [2002], Liu described his results at the annual meeting of the American Association for the Advancement of Science in Washington, D.C.

"It's the first time we've been able to peer back before the historical record to see how hurricanes vary in time," says Kerry A. Emanuel of the Massachusetts Institute of Technology, who would like to use such data to test whether the anticipated global warming will increase the number of severe hurricanes.

Scientists aren't alone in taking an interest in paleotempestology. Most of the field's funding comes from the Risk Prediction Initiative, an effort bankrolled by insurance companies in need of better data with which to predict the odds of a severe hurricane landfall in a specific region. Considering that category 4 and 5 hurricanes can cause billions of dollars in damage, the future of these insurance companies may rest on the accuracy of their estimates.

Paleotempestology "is a nice scientific challenge, but it's [also] got a very practical outcome," notes Thompson Webb III of

Brown University in Providence, R.I., who has conducted work similar to Liu's.

When the category 4 hurricane ripped through Galveston in 1900, wind and rain alone produced significant damage and some loss of life. But as in many such tempests, the real killer was the flooding by the storm surge. Hurricane winds blowing over shallows near a coastline can raise up a dome of salt water 50 to 100 miles across. This storm surge can send up to 25 feet of water into the region where a hurricane makes landfall.

If a lake or marsh sits not far from the coast, the storm surge may also leave an enduring imprint of the hurricane. Sand from the ocean floor or beach can be thrown inland with the water, eventually settling to the bottom of the lakes or marshes in a discernible sediment layer that records the storm's impact.

In 1990, Liu and his graduate student Miriam L. Fearn began to look for such sand layers at Lake Shelby, just off the Alabama coast. They drilled into the lake bottom, removing cores of sediment ranging from 1 to 10 meters deep.

A category 3 hurricane called Frederic had run through that region in 1979. In cores taken on the edge of the lake nearest the coast, the two investigators found a surface stratum of sand, which they attributed to Frederic. Cores taken in the middle of the lake didn't contain this recent layer, indicating that the hurricane wasn't fierce enough to send sand that far into the lake. Those cores did, however, hold 11 other sand layers, 0.1 to 1 centimeter thick, which Liu and Fearn concluded could only have resulted from the storm surges of earlier category 4 or 5 hurricanes.

"There are no other high-energy events that would cause sand to be transported out into the middle of a lake," contends Liu.

Through dating methods such as radiocarbon analysis of organic matter within the cores, the scientists were able to determine that nine of the lake's sand layers originated between 2,200 and 3,300 years ago. The two more recent millennia each had one sand layer.

Over the past decade, Liu and his colleagues have drilled similar cores in 16 lakes and marshes along the Gulf Coast from Texas to Florida. For four of the sites—Pearl River Marsh in Louisiana, Pascagoula Marsh in Mississippi, Lake Shelby in Alabama, and Western Lake in Florida—the investigators obtained sediment cores going back about 5,000 years.

The historical record of the past 150 years clearly indicates that total hurricane activity along the U.S. coast varies decade by decade. When Liu's team lined up their cores from the four sites, they realized that catastrophic storm activity rises and falls over longer periods, as well.

"There are millennial-scale variations in hurricane activity. Our data suggest that there are much longer cycles superimposed on the decadal cycles," says Liu. "We've had a quiet period, an active period, and for the past 1,000 years, we're back to a relatively quiet period."

Indeed, the data indicate that catastrophic hurricanes struck the Gulf Coast much more frequently 1,000 to 3,500 years ago than they do now. During that hyperactive period, such storms hit the area from four to five times more often than they have in the past 1,000 years.

Combining the data on the past 3,500 years from several of their sites, the investigators conclude that a category 4 or 5 hurricane batters the Gulf Coast every 300 or so years. In other words, there's about a 0.3 percent chance each year that the region will see a storm like the one that razed Galveston in 1900—or something even stronger.

This is the first time that scientists can provide insurance companies with an estimate of severe hurricane frequency that has any compelling data to back it up, says Liu.

There was some initial skepticism that the sand layers observed in Liu's coastal lake cores were truly from storm surges caused by ancient hurricanes. As his team has studied additional sites, other scientists have grown more comfortable with the strategy.

"I feel pretty confident that they're seeing a storm record. There's no other way to explain how you get a big sand layer," says David L. Malmquist of the Bermuda Biological Station for Research in St. George's, who heads the Risk Prediction Initiative.

It also helps that another research team has tried Liu's strategy and is having similar success. During the past few years, Webb and Jeff Donnelly, also at Brown University, have led an effort to draw cores from coastal salt marshes in Rhode Island, New Jersey, Massachusetts, and Connecticut. While their cores push only 600 to 1,000 years into the past, the scientists have matched many of their sand layers to hurricanes documented in the historical record.

"It was key to prove the method with known storms," says Webb.

Paleotempestology may help insurance companies better set

their rates, but scientists also desire the field's data to learn how climate influences hurricane activity. For example, what climatic changes could have caused the millennial shifts in hurricane activity along the Gulf Coast revealed by the cores?

Liu hypothesizes that the shifting position of the Bermuda high explains the change in landfall frequency along the Gulf. A region of high atmospheric pressure in which air circulates clockwise, the Bermuda high has a strong influence on the climate of North America.

Scientists, for example, have attributed changing precipitation patterns in the United States over the past 10,000 years to shifts in the Bermuda high's position. The central and the eastern parts of the country seesaw back and forth in receiving the greater amount of rain.

Liu suggests that his ancient hurricanes also follow an alternating pattern based on the Bermuda high. "If the high-pressure system is situated close to the continent and the Caribbean, then hurricanes tend to get steered to the Gulf Coast," explains Liu. If the Bermuda high sits far from North America, hurricanes instead usually head for the Atlantic coastline.

He's now compiling coring data from sites in Virginia and Massachusetts to determine if ancient hurricane activity rises along the Atlantic Coast when it declines in the Gulf.

"The data so far show potential for supporting the hypothesis, but we need to do much more work," says Liu.

Beyond looking for sand layers caused by storm surges, scientists are investigating novel ways to document ancient hurricanes. Liu, for example, has traveled across the Pacific Ocean—where hurricanes are usually called typhoons or cyclones—in an attempt to extend the historical record.

"In China, there are very good records kept at the county level. County gazettes record every significant cultural and natural event in the area," he notes.

In a pilot project using the records of a province near Hong Kong, Liu has compiled a 1,000-year record of typhoon landfalls. It reveals variations in hurricane frequency on the scale of centuries as well as decades.

That success has prompted the National Science Foundation to fund a project that will explore the gazettes from provinces all along the China coast.

"This will be the longest tropical cyclone record in the world," says Liu, who further hopes to take cores from coastal lakes in China to corroborate the hurricanes recorded in the gazettes.

There are also options other than sand layers and paper records. Scientists are considering coral, tree rings, pollen, caves, and even clam shells as indicators of cyclones.

A research team led by Bjorn Malmgren at the University of Gsteborg in Sweden has begun to study the humic-acid content of coral from sites in the Caribbean. Humic acids in soil run off into the ocean during the heavy rainfalls of severe hurricanes, and corals incorporate the acids into their skeletons. Malmgren says that by measuring how the humic-acid content of corals varies with time, his group can develop a record of ancient tropical cyclones.

The fierce winds of major hurricanes can also shear off the crowns of tall trees, reducing their photosynthetic ability. The resulting reduction in growth rate shows up as thin tree rings.

Similarly, the destruction caused by catastrophic hurricanes can change the vegetation within a region for years, altering the kinds and quantities of pollen trapped in sediments of lakes, ponds, and marshes. Other phenomena that affect the pollen record, such as fires or human deforestation, complicate its use in identifying prehistoric hurricanes, however.

One of the more unusual, and unexplained, features of a hurricane is that its rain is isotopically lighter than normal, with a lower concentration of oxygen 18 than typical rainwater has. James R. Lawrence of the University of Houston made this discovery in 1989 while studying groundwater after a Texas hurricane. He and other scientists propose that hurricane rainfall seeping into caves may be incorporated as detectable layers within deposits such as stalagmites or stalactites. Lawrence has also suggested studying clams to see if the carbonate in their shells holds an isotopic record of hurricane rain.

Despite these efforts, the search for signs of ancient hurricanes remains in its infancy. "One of the problems with paleotempestology is getting it jump-started," says Emanuel. "There's just a handful of people doing this."

That's in large part, he adds, because federal agencies haven't embraced the interdisciplinary field, leaving the Risk Prediction Initiative as almost the only source of funding.

Yet to understand how a changing climate influences the number and intensity of hurricanes, scientists must turn to paleotempestology, argues Emanuel. He notes that predictions made by climate models on this issue don't inspire confidence. One model suggests that global warming will increase hurricane frequency, while another foretells the exact opposite.

"I don't think there's any other way we're going to get a handle on the relationship between hurricanes and climate except by looking back in time," concludes Emanuel.

# The Possibility of Ancient "Hypercanes"

## By Kathy A. Svitil

*Some researchers have theorized that severe hurricane activity could have led to the extinction of the dinosaurs, writes Kathy A. Svitil in the following selection. According to atmospheric scientist Kerry Emanuel, an asteroid slamming into the ocean would have released intense heat, warming surrounding waters to high temperatures that could have produced a "hypercane"—a twenty-mile-high storm with five hundred miles-per-hour winds. Hypercanes might have damaged the ozone layer, Svitil reports; they may also have released massive dust clouds that blocked out the sun, destroying most animal life. Svitil is an associate editor of* Discover, *a monthly science magazine.*

Most researchers believe a large asteroid or comet smacked into Earth around 65 million years ago, killing off the dinosaurs and three-quarters of the other species. They even know where ground zero was: the northern coast of Mexico's Yucatan Peninsula, where a large sediment-filled crater straddles the land and sea. What nobody is sure of, however, is how such an impact might have killed so widely. The conventional wisdom is that the impact—or volcanic eruptions triggered by the impact—launched a global pall of dust and gases that blocked out the sun or wiped out the ozone layer or both. But no one, says atmospheric scientist Kerry Emanuel of MIT [Massachusetts Institute of Technology] has been able to explain exactly how all that stuff got up into the stratosphere—10 to 35 miles above the surface—which it would have to do if

Kathy A. Svitil, "Hurricane from Hell," *Discover*, vol. 16, April 1995, p. 26. Copyright © 1995 by Kathy A. Svitil. Reproduced by permission.

# A Total Dissolution of Nature

### BY ALEXANDER HAMILTON

*The following selection, a letter written by a teenaged Alexander Hamilton to his father, is an impressionistic account of a hurricane that struck St. Croix, Virgin Islands, in August 1772. He sent the letter to the island's newspaper, which published it a week after the storm. From Hamilton's description, it appears that the hurricane's eye passed directly over the island. Hamilton wonders if the hurricane is an expression of God's wrath, and alternately expresses terror and relief, elation and humility. In the end, he implores the affluent to help those whom the storm left poor, sick, and wounded. Hamilton eventually became an American Revolutionary War hero and the first U.S. secretary of the treasury.*

Honoured Sir,—I take up my pen just to give you an imperfect account of the most dreadful hurricane that memory or any records whatever can trace, which happened here on the 31st ultimo at night.

It began about dusk, at North, and raged very violently till ten o'clock. Then ensued a sudden and unexpected interval, which lasted about an hour. Meanwhile the wind was shifting round to the South West point, from whence it returned with redoubled fury and continued so till near three o'clock in the morning. Good God! what horror and destruction—it's impossible for me to describe—or you to form any idea of it. It seemed as if a total dissolution of nature was taking place. The roaring of the sea and wind—fiery meteors flying about in the air—the prodigious glare of almost perpetual lightning—the crash of the falling

Alexander Hamilton, "St. Croix, September 6, 1772," *A Few of Hamilton's Letters: Including His Description of the Great West Indian Hurricane of 1772*, edited by Gertrude Atherton. New York: The Macmillan Company, 1903.

it were to spread all over the planet. Now Emanuel and a team of colleagues think they've found the answer. It's still purely hypothetical, and that is fortunate. A hypercane, as they call their creation, would be a hurricane we'd never want to see.

## A Phenomenal Storm

"We were trying to predict the maximum intensity that ordinary hurricanes could reach," says Emanuel. "And we noticed that if we made the ocean too warm and the atmosphere too cold, the equation didn't yield any sensible solution—it kind of blew up." Unable to solve the problem with pencil and paper, Emanuel and his colleagues ran a computer simulation of a hurricane over a pool of hot ocean. The computer spat out a phenomenal storm—20 miles high, with winds approaching 500 miles an hour.

The water that created this hypercane was so hot—120 degrees at the center of the pool—that the team knew such a storm couldn't occur in the present climate "or in any climates that Earth had experienced, except maybe near its origin," Emanuel says. "But we thought that under extraordinary circumstances one might have observed such a storm." A large asteroid or comet slamming into the ocean floor, for instance, would release a lot of heat. If an area of ocean at least 30 miles across were heated to around 120 degrees, Emanuel and his colleagues have found, the result would be a hypercane.

An ordinary hurricane forms over a much larger region of the ocean, and one that has been baked to a much lower temperature by the sun. The warm water heats the air above it, and as that warm air begins to rise, it creates a low-pressure zone that draws in air from all sides. The wind causes more water to evaporate, which transfers more heat to the air, which accelerates the nascent storm—and since Earth is spinning, the storm spins, too.

In an ordinary hurricane, friction exerted by the sea on the swirling winds limits their speed to 200 miles an hour or less. But in a hypercane, that control is overwhelmed by the tremendous heat of the impact, which keeps pumping energy into the storm. "The heat engine of the hurricane just runs away," Emanuel says. "Friction can't keep up with it." The winds accelerate to 500 miles an hour. Because the angular momentum of the storm must stay the same, it shrinks to a tight knot just 10 miles across—around a sixth of the diameter of an ordinary hurricane.

Meanwhile it is growing to twice the height, 20 miles high or so, because the air in its center is so hot: that air must rise until it has cooled to the temperature of the air around it. The result is a storm tall enough and strong enough to catapult a huge amount of material—water vapor, sea salt, and maybe dust, if the crater happened to nick a coastline, as it did in the Yucatan—well into the stratosphere.

## A Cause of Extinction?

The water vapor or chlorine released by the sea salt could have triggered reactions that destroyed the ozone layer, exposing the animals below to withering ultraviolet radiation; the dust could have frozen and starved them by blocking out the sun. Emanuel and his colleagues aren't sure which disaster befell the dinosaurs. But a single hypercane, they know, wouldn't have done the trick—it would have taken a series. "A hypercane could only exist over very hot water," Emanuel explains, "and as soon as it moved off that hot water—carried by the background flow of the atmosphere—it would then turn into a normal hurricane. So you could get a sequence of these things—one would develop and move off downwind, and then another would develop over the hot water. If that sequence lasted more than a week, it could have dramatic global effects."

# Disasters and Personal Accounts

houses—and the ear-piercing shrieks of the distressed, were sufficient to strike astonishment into Angels. A great part of the buildings throughout the Island are levelled to the ground—almost all the rest very much shattered—several persons killed and numbers utterly ruined—whole families running about the streets unknowing where to find a place of shelter—the sick exposed to the keenness of water and air—without a bed to lie upon—or a dry covering to their bodies—our harbour is entirely bare. In a word, misery in all its most hideous shapes spread over the whole face of the country.—A strong smell of gunpowder added somewhat to the terrors of the night; and it was observed that the rain was surprisingly salt. Indeed, the water is so brackish and full of sulphur that there is hardly any drinking it.

My reflections and feelings on this frightful and melancholy occasion are set forth in following self-discourse.

## Humble and Helpless

Where now, Oh! vile worm, is all thy boasted fortitude and resolution? what is become of thy arrogance and self-sufficiency?—why dost thou tremble and stand aghast? how humble—how helpless—how contemptible you now appear. And for why? the jarring of the elements—the discord of clouds? Oh, impotent presumptuous fool! how darest thou offend that omnipotence, whose nod alone were sufficient to quell the destruction that hovers over thee, or crush thee into atoms? See thy wretched helpless state and learn to know thyself. Learn to know thy best support. Despise thyself and adore thy God. How sweet—how unutterably sweet were now the voice of an approving conscience;—then couldst thou say—hence ye idle alarms—why do I shrink? What have I to fear? A pleasing calm suspense! a short repose from calamity to end in eternal bliss?—let the earth rend, let the planets forsake their course—let the sun be extinguished, and the heavens burst asunder—yet what have I to dread? my staff can never be broken—in omnipotence I trust.

He who gave the winds to blow and the lightnings to rage—even him I have always loved and served—his precepts have I observed—his commandments have I obeyed—and his perfections have I adored.—He will snatch me from ruin—he will exalt me to the fellowship of Angels and Seraphs, and to the fulness of never ending joys.

But alas! how different, how deplorable—how gloomy the

prospect—death comes rushing on in triumph veiled in a mantle of ten-fold darkness. His unrelenting scythe, pointed and ready for the stroke.—On his right hand sits destruction, hurling the winds and belching forth flames;—calamity on his left threatening famine, disease, distress of all kinds.—And Oh! thou wretch, look still a little further; see the gulf of eternal mystery open—there mayest thou shortly plunge—the just reward of thy vileness.—Alas! whither canst thou fly? where hide thyself? thou canst not call upon thy God;—thy life has been a continual warfare with him.

Hark! ruin and confusion on every side.—'Tis thy turn next: but one short moment—even now—Oh Lord help—Jesus be merciful!

## Distress and Terror

Thus did I reflect, and thus at every gust of the wind did I conclude,—till it pleased the Almighty to allay it.—Nor did my emotions proceed either from the suggestion of too much natural fear, or a conscience overburdened with crimes of an uncommon cast.—I thank God this was not the case. The scenes of horror exhibited around us, naturally awakened such ideas in every thinking breast, and aggravated the deformity of every failing of our lives. It were a lamentable insensibility indeed, not to have had such feelings,—and I think inconsistent with human nature.

Our distressed helpless condition taught us humility and a contempt of ourselves.—The horrors of the night—the prospect of an immediate cruel death—or, as one may say, of being crushed by the Almighty in his anger—filled us with terror. And everything that had tended to weaken our interest with Him, upbraided us, in the strongest colours, with our baseness and folly.—That which, in a calm unruffled temper, we call a natural cause, seemed then like the correction of the Deity.— Our imagination represented him as an incensed master, executing vengeance on the crimes of his servants.—The father and benefactor were forgot, and in that view, a consciousness of our guilt filled us with despair.

But see, the Lord relents—he hears our prayers—the Lightning ceases—the winds are appeased—the warring elements are reconciled, and all things promise peace.—The darkness is dispelled— and drooping nature revives at the approaching dawn. Look back, Oh, my soul—look back and tremble.—Rejoice at thy deliverance, and humble thyself in the presence of thy deliverer.

# Sights of Woe

Yet hold, Oh, vain mortal!—check thy ill-timed joy. Art thou so selfish as to exult because thy lot is happy in a season of universal woe?—Hast thou no feelings for the miseries of thy fellow-creatures, and art thou incapable of the soft pangs of sympathetic sorrow?—Look around thee and shudder at the view.—See desolation and ruin wherever thou turnest thine eye. See thy fellow-creatures pale and lifeless; their bodies mangled—their souls snatched into eternity—unexpecting—alas! perhaps unprepared!—Hark the bitter groans of distress—see sickness and infirmities exposed to the inclemencies of wind and water—see tender infancy pinched with hunger and hanging to the mother's knee for food!—see the unhappy mother's anxiety—her poverty denies relief—her breast heaves with pangs of maternal pity—her heart is bursting—the tears gush down her cheeks—Oh sights of woe! Oh distress unspeakable—my heart bleeds—but I have no power to solace!—Oh ye, who revel in affluence, see the afflictions of humanity, and bestow your superfluity to ease them.—Say not, we have suffered also, and with-hold your compassion. What are your sufferings compared to these? Ye have still more than enough left.—Act wisely.—Succour the miserable and lay up a treasure in Heaven.

I am afraid, sir, you will think this description more the effort of imagination, than a true picture of realities. But I can affirm with the greatest truth, that there is not a single circumstance touched upon which I have not absolutely been an eye-witness to.

# The Great Galveston Hurricane of 1900

## BY STEPHEN FOX

*The deadliest U.S. hurricane on record—and the country's worst natural disaster—is the category 4 storm that hit Galveston, Texas, on September 8, 1900. Emerging from the Caribbean Sea, it moved across Cuba and quickly strengthened as it headed north. Weather experts thought the storm would continue on a northerly track and hit the nation's eastern seaboard, but it unexpectedly turned west, crossing the Gulf of Mexico before slamming into the east coast of Texas. Galveston, a cosmopolitan resort situated on a barrier island just off of the mainland, was especially vulnerable because of its low altitude and unsheltered beaches. The storm killed at least eight thousand people and destroyed one-third of the city's houses and streets. In the following selection, Stephen Fox, a historian and biographer who lives near Boston, Massachusetts, describes the destruction wrought by the Galveston hurricane. He focuses on the perspective of Isaac Cline, head of the city's weather bureau, who tried to warn beachgoers of the impending storm. Cline and many others exerted heroic efforts to survive and save lives during the height of the hurricane.*

The dedicated weatherman and the terrible storm collided during the first week of September 1900. Isaac Cline, head of the U.S. Weather Bureau station in Galveston, Texas, was tracking a hurricane headed northwest through the Caribbean. Cline was fascinated by the young science of meteorology; after 18 years in the Weather Bureau, the last 11 in Galveston, he knew his field well. He expected this particular tropical cyclone, once it passed across Cuba, to run up the Eastern Seaboard of the United States. But it hit a stubborn high-

Stephen Fox, "'For a While . . . It Was Fun,' Then the Full Force of the Storm Hit," *Smithsonian*, September 1999, p. 128. Copyright © 1999 by Stephen Fox. Reproduced by permission of the author.

pressure block over Florida and veered west. The last information Cline received placed the storm south of Louisiana as it screamed across the Gulf of Mexico toward Galveston.

In the roll call of America's deadliest disasters, the body count becomes a grim Richter scale. Think of the 250 people killed in the Chicago fire of 1871, the 1,182 in the forest fire at Peshtigo, Wisconsin, in that same year, the 503 in the San Francisco earthquake of 1906, and then, even worse, the 1,836 lost in the Florida hurricane of 1928, and the 2,209 in the Johnstown flood of 1889. Yet the total deaths from these five catastrophes, taken together, amount to thousands fewer than the toll inflicted by the Galveston hurricane [of 1900].

# A Place Apart

It seemed obvious, afterward, that Galveston was vulnerable to calamity. The city perched on the eastern end of a barrier island— an exaggerated sandbar—a few miles off the Texas coast. Its main street, Broadway, bisected the city along the island's spine from northeast to southwest. At only 8.7 feet above sea level, Broadway offered the highest land in Galveston. Facing the Gulf, a wide, level beach ran the length of the island—27 miles of glistening white sand. To improve beach access, protective sand dunes up to 15 feet high had been removed along the city's edge. A traveler approaching Galveston from the Gulf first glimpsed its buildings seemingly floating in water, miragelike, with no land in sight.

Geography had made the place both attractive and dangerous. Constant sea breezes kept its summer weather more temperate than on the neighboring Texas mainland, drawing thousands of visitors. On the north side of town, on Galveston Bay, a new deepwater harbor promised a prosperous future. The federal government had recently spent $7 million on dredging and building jetties to deepen the channel from the Gulf into the bay. The harbor's cotton and grain exports had made Galveston, linked by railroad bridges to the mainland, the major banking and financial center between New Orleans and San Francisco. Impressive Victorian mansions were sprouting along Broadway, and new residential areas were spreading to the south and west, toward the unsheltered beach.

As resort, port and mercantile center, Galveston radiated a cosmopolitan ease. It included many citizens of German, French, Jewish and Italian ancestry, the first synagogue in Texas, and the

seat of the state's oldest Roman Catholic diocese. The three leading Galveston merchant families were Protestant, Protestant, and
Jewish. About 22 percent of the population was black. With
power so diffused, nobody really dominated. The Artillery Club,
formal and exclusive, lay adjacent to the fanciest whorehouse in
town. People came to Galveston to enjoy themselves amid the
oleanders and public gardens. Young swells took to oyster roasts,
boat sails and fishing parties. For other tastes there were a dozen
public gambling houses and many unregulated saloons that never
closed. Bathhouses and refreshment stands lined the beach. Nude
bathing, popular with both men and women, was restricted by
city ordinance to late at night.

It was a place apart. Insularity bred both pride and complacency. At regular intervals, and particularly in 1875 and 1886,
high water had swept over Galveston. These "overflows" were accepted as part of the island's uniqueness; with no great damage
done, residents mopped up, cracked jokes and went on as before.
Sensible proposals to build a protective dike around the city had
gone nowhere. The famous beach sloped off to deep water so
gradually that (it was understood) destructive waves from the Gulf
would surely break and be spent before reaching shore.

## Isaac Cline

Isaac Cline, not a native, had his doubts. Thirty-eight years old at
the time of the storm, he had grown up on a Tennessee farm and
after college joined the agency that would become the Weather
Bureau. While rising through various postings, he also earned a
medical degree in order to study weather's effects on the human
body, published and edited a newspaper, campaigned for tem-
perance, and finished another doctorate, in philosophy and soci-
ology. Cline met his wife, Cora, at the Baptist church where she
served as organist. They had three young daughters, and Cora was
well into her fourth pregnancy. Given Galveston's history of overflows and hurricanes, Isaac Cline had built his family an exceptionally strong frame house a few blocks from the beach, with the
first floor built above the high water mark of 1875.

On Friday, September 7, he scanned the sky over the Gulf. For
several days, he had been receiving storm-warning advisories from
the Weather Bureau's headquarters in Washington, D.C. He had
not observed, however, any of "the usual signs which herald the
approach of hurricane" he later wrote in a report on the storm.

He saw no "brick-dust sky," usually a reliable clue to approaching hurricanes in that area. Barometric pressure had fallen only slightly. The first real harbinger, a heavy swell from the southeast, arrived in the afternoon and continued through the night. The tide rose unusually high despite fighting strong opposing winds from the north and northwest.

At 4 o'clock Saturday morning, Cline's younger brother Joe, who roomed with the Clines and also worked at the weather office, awoke with an inexplicable sense of impending disaster. The backyard, he saw, was flooded. Alerted by his brother, Isaac drove his horse and wagon to the Gulf, where he timed the swells, and then went to his office in the city's commercial section. He found the barometer had dipped only a tenth of an inch since 8:00 p.m. the night before. He returned to the beach to gauge the tide and swells again before sending a telegram to Washington: "Unusually heavy swells from the southeast, intervals one to five minutes, overflowing low places south portion of city three to four blocks from beach. Such high water with opposing winds never observed previously." Again he went back to the beach, warning people to move inland to find shelter.

## Fun for a While

Light showers fell during the forenoon but didn't prevent thousands of people in fancy clothes from visiting the beach to watch the booming, crashing surf. Some even went swimming. Children played with driftwood boats in the flooded streets. "For a while," Louisa Christine Rollfing recalled, "even ladies were wading in the water, thinking it was fun. The children had a grand time." A holiday spirit persisted until the bathhouses, extended into the Gulf on pilings, broke apart. Then the streetcars stopped running. Moods and skies began to darken. ("Then it wasn't fun any more," Rollfing noted.)

A heavy, persistent rain started around noon as the barometer plummeted and winds grew stronger. The hurricane was aiming dead at Galveston. All bridges to the mainland were underwater. Boats were useless in such conditions. No one could leave the island. The city's telephone, electric and gas utilities blinked out. People waded and swam away from the encroaching surf toward the slightly higher ground midtown. "The Gulf," Katherine Vedder Pauls said years later, "looked like a great gray wall about 50 feet high and moving slowly toward the island." Finally sensing

danger, with the hurricane bearing down on them, Galvestonians were trapped on their sandbar.

At midafternoon Isaac Cline waded nearly two miles to home.
The air was filled with flying bricks, masonry, roof slates, timbers,
even entire roofs. Dodging those missiles, Cline also skirted
downed electric wires, some sputtering and burning like long,
sulfurous snakes. At home he found the water around his house
waist deep. About 50 neighbors crowded in, drawn by the house's
sturdy construction. When Joe arrived, the brothers stepped outside. Should they seek shelter inland? Isaac was loath to move
Cora, pregnant and ill at the time. Aside from the wind and water, the airborne debris might harm his three little girls. The
house was built to stand. A sudden rise in water forced the decision to stay put.

## Desperate Dramas

Thousands of desperate individual dramas unfolded. Henry
Johnson, a black laborer recently arrived in Galveston, took refuge
in his boardinghouse near the center of town. The wind rocked
the house back and forth "like a barrel," Johnson remembered.
When the back porch collapsed, with the house likely to follow,
he fled outside. Neighborhood men helped people leave by pushing clumps of debris out of the way with long poles. White or
black. Johnson said later, it made no difference; everyone was
treated alike in the crisis. Someone took him to the Union Railroad Passenger Depot, a substantial public building. It was already
crowded with refugees and their animals. For hours people kept
straggling in, many naked and bleeding, with broken arms, some
crying a wild gibberish. Windows broke but somehow the depot
itself held.

Giuseppe and Concetta Rizzo, immigrants from Italy, lived
near the beach in the east end of town. Their grandson, Jimmy
La Coume, a lifelong Galvestonian now [more than 70] years old,
recounts the story as it has passed down through the family. One
of Giuseppe's brothers came to the house in a rowboat. He only
had room for Concetta and her daughter, Jimmy's mother, then
7 years old. "OK," said Giuseppe, "come back for me." Before the
boat could return, the house was swept away and Giuseppe was
lost. Concetta and her daughter went to the nearby Sacred Heart
Church, where the dome soon collapsed, and then to Saint
Mary's University where, on the second floor, they rode out the

storm, wondering about Giuseppe's fate.

Terrifying sounds came in relentless waves and pulses. The wind shrieked and whistled, driving the rain and groundwater. Whitecapped waves six feet high coursed up Broadway. The slanting rain, cold and sharp, felt like needles or glass splinters in the face. When slate shingles were torn off a roof, to the people cowering inside, it sounded like a freight train passing over the house. The buildings themselves seemed to be crying amid the cacophony of breaking glass, falling walls, rattling tin roofs, and wooden rain cisterns rolling and tumbling. The spire of St. Patrick's Church, the tallest structure on the island, rocked and swayed for hours, then fell in a wind gust so loud that nobody heard the tower crash. In momentary lulls even more terrible sounds became audible: cries for help, usually unanswered and unanswerable, from the dying and drowning.

The storm leveled all social distinctions, but it could not erase all cultural differences. The wife of Clarence Ousley, editor of the *Galveston Tribune*, had never truly accepted her neighbors the Niccolinis because—as Ousley's daughter Angie later put it—"they spoke English with difficulty and also used a trifle too much garlic in their cooking." The Niccolinis, "all extremely vocal," arrived seeking shelter. The Ousleys gave them a bedroom of their own.

A few blocks from Isaac Cline's house, the Ursuline Convent and Academy took in nearly a thousand refugees. When part of the north wall fell in, about a hundred blacks started to shout and sing in "camp meeting" style. Whites unaccustomed to this kind of worship grew restive and irritated. Tempers, drawn so taut, started fraying. Mother Superioress Joseph rang the chapel bell, hushed the crowd, and told them that God would hear their silent prayers, from their hearts, even through the hurricane. Everyone settled down to endure the storm together.

Shortly after 5 o'clock, the anemometer at the Weather Bureau recorded gusts of 100 miles an hour, then blew away. Isaac Cline later guessed the wind peaked at 120 miles an hour. George Mc-Neir, captain of the sloop Cora Dean in Galveston Harbor, was sure it actually hit 150 miles an hour. When McNeir went aloft to clear mastheads in the ship's rigging, a tremendous gust of wind tore his feet from the lines and hung him out horizontally, like a pennant, until the gust subsided and he could continue climbing.

## The Crest of the Storm

The hurricane crested in the early evening. "As darkness came on," Walter Davis later wrote his mother, "the Terror increased." With the storm roaring at its height, and no electricity or gas, people relied on candles and kerosene lanterns—and occasional flashes of lightning—to see by. Otherwise the blackness was complete, adding visual isolation to already-desperate straits. The wind shifted to northeast and then east, reinforcing the building tide from the Gulf. A massive storm wave broke on the island. At 8:30 the barometer bottomed out at 28.48 inches, the lowest pressure recorded up to that time at any Weather Bureau station.

Floating clumps of wreckage, joining and separating, careened around and slammed into buildings. The Cline house held up under this fearsome battering until Isaac, bunkered with his family on the second floor, saw a long piece of streetcar trestle crash squarely against the side of his home. The house creaked, tipped over into the water and started breaking into pieces. Joe Cline, holding his two older nieces by their hands, turned his back toward a window, pushed from his heels, and broke through the glass and storm shutters. They found themselves floating on a piece of the house. No other survivors could be seen.

Isaac, Cora and their youngest daughter were thrown against

*The Galveston Hurricane of 1900 killed more than eight thousand people and destroyed one-third of the city's homes and streets.*

a chimney, then into the bottom of the wreckage. Isaac, pinned down, expected to die. "It is useless to fight for life," he remembered thinking. "I will let the water enter my lungs and pass on." He lost consciousness; but by some mysterious shifting of the ruins he was propelled upward and came to with his body wedged between heavy floating timbers. During a flash of lightning he caught sight of his youngest girl on wreckage a few feet away. A few minutes later, another flash revealed Joe and the other children. Cora was gone, somewhere down below. The surviving Clines struggled onto the best piece of flotsam they could find.

For the next three hours they drifted out of control, switching from clump to clump as their fragile rafts broke apart. Placing the children in front of them, the men turned their backs to the wind, holding up planks for puny shelter. Still they were repeatedly hit and bloodied. An especially heavy blow would knock them into the water and they would struggle back to the children.

At one point, by a miracle beyond explanation, the family dog—a fine hunting retriever—appeared from nowhere and clawed his way onto the wreckage. The dog frantically smelled each of the Clines and, unsatisfied, dashed to the edge. To Joe it seemed that he was looking for Cora. The dog poised to jump and resume his hopeless search; Joe shouted and lunged for him, but he darted away and was gone. "I can almost believe to this day that animals have superhuman senses in time of danger." Joe wrote years later. "We never saw him any more."

## Heroic Efforts

Both humans and animals performed heroic feats under pressure. Daniel Ransom, a paperhanger and a strong swimmer, spent 2½ hours in the water, leading and carrying 45 people to safety at a large brick building. At Saint Mary's Infirmary, Joseph Corthell, a harbor pilot, and his brothers used a lifeboat to ferry more than 150 people from the neighborhood to the hospital—until their boat sank. Also at Saint Mary's, a medical student, Zachary Scott, carried more than 200 patients from outbuildings to the main structure, wading through water that eventually reached a depth of six feet.

Each hero had to make the essential fateful decision: whether to hang back in self-preservation or dare the howling maelstrom, at grave personal risk, to try to save others. Harry Maxson, 14 years old, lived with his family on the west side of town. Their house was the last remaining refuge in the neighborhood. Late that night, during a lull, Harry raised a kitchen window and listened. "I heard what I didn't want to hear," he wrote years later, "a woman yelling 'for God Sake come and save us, our home is falling to pieces.' I shut the window as quickly as I could and tried to forget that woman's voice. It was awful so far away and still so penetrating; it made me shake all over." In the next lull he opened the window again and heard the voice cry, "I can see the lights in your house." That brought it home: he had to go.

Harry told his father but could not bear to say goodbye to his mother, and set out with another man. They rode the waves toward the woman's house, which was floating and breaking apart. Inside were 13 children and 23 adults. Harry shouted that they would take the kids first, calling on each man in the house to accompany them with one child. "The longest silence I ever heard," Harry recalled, "but no one came out or even said 'boo,' . . . The men in the house were paralyzed with fear." At last a large black man appeared with a white baby, followed by the other men carrying children and some of their wives. They struggled single file, each man holding on to the next, to the Maxson house. Harry and several men undertook another trip to rescue those who remained.

The Clines drifted out to sea. They saw no houses, lights or people for two hours. Then the wind shifted to the south and blew them back to shore; they landed only 300 yards from where they had started. All were frightfully bruised; one of the girls was barely alive. They dragged themselves into a house with no roof or ceiling, and collapsed for the night, bone-weary and hurting.

## The Aftermath

Sunday arrived with a beautiful sunrise and calm ocean. As survivors crawled out, looked around and got their bearings, the magnitude of the disaster was slowly revealed. It was too much to take in quickly. "There was little talk." Katherine Vedder Pauls recalled. "All were stunned by the catastrophe." About one-third of the city, mostly in sections near the Gulf, was completely gone; no houses or even streets were left, only scoured sand. Along the upper edge of that vast emptiness, a three-mile window of wreckage, up to two stories high and 100 feet thick, had been formed: a mass of lumber, debris and mangled corpses. In the rest of the city, hardly a building was left undamaged, and many had disappeared altogether. More than 3,600 houses were destroyed.

The retreating water left a thick slime, rank and penetrating. In the harbor, the steamship Roma had torn loose from its mooring, crashed into two large piers, smashed broadside through all three railroad bridges and lay stranded in mud. Docks, warehouses and grain elevators were wrecked or severely damaged. Boats of all sizes were scattered around. With telephone and telegraph wires down, one of the few boats still seaworthy was dispatched to the mainland bearing the first grim news.

Bodies, torn and naked, were everywhere; in yards and streets, caught in trees and random structures, floating in the bay. "Put your foot down." Henry Johnson recalled, "an' you put it on a dead man." Some kept their children indoors to avoid the searing sights. In one house, 13 of 15 people had died. One family lost 28 relatives; another, 42. "Every one here seems stunned." Eleanor Hertford wrote her future husband, "and you never see any emotion displayed of any kind, every one is perfectly calm! We all seem to have gone through so much, that we seem beyond tears!" Survivors told each other matter-of-factly of crushing family losses. "All gone," they said, all gone.

The first estimate on Sunday was 500 dead. Bodies were borne on stretchers to temporary morgues. As corpses kept turning up, the estimate went to 3,000. The saturated ground prevented mass burial. Polite formalities had to be suspended; bodies were piled on wagons without ceremony, taken to barges and dumped at sea. When they floated back to shore, immediate cremation became necessary. (In the 80-degree weather, the foul stench of putrefying flesh quickly became overwhelming.) For a month, about 70 bodies a day were found among the piles of wreckage. Most of them were simply doused with oil and burned on the spot with the debris. The soundest contemporary estimate placed the final toll at 6,000 in Galveston, a thousand elsewhere on the island, and another thousand on the mainland: a total of at least 8,000 dead, a figure accepted in recent years in studies published by the National Oceanic and Atmospheric Administration.

In the immediate chaos that followed the storm, some looting took place. Giuseppe Rizzo's body was found with $500 missing from his money belt. An emergency guard force was soon overwhelmed. Robbers pillaged through property, staged daylight holdups, and cut the ears and swollen fingers from corpses for the jewelry. Looters were shot on sight; perhaps a dozen, perhaps scores. No records were kept. "Tuesday I went round with a pistol," Sarah Davis Hawley wrote her mother, "as so many people had been killed while trying to protect their things. And you can never realize the awfulness of it all." Gunfire punctuated the nights. Reports of looting continued until Thursday, five days after the hurricane, when martial law was officially imposed to restore order to the city.

## Absorbing the Losses

Several days after the storm, Ella Sealy Newell heard a boy whistling. "We all stopped to listen," she noted. "It was the first joyous sound we had heard; anything gay or bright in dress, or manner, seems utterly out of place." As time passed, most Galvestonians absorbed their losses, picked through the debris and resumed living. Isaac Cline, with Cora still missing, went back to work with his head bandaged and a foot poulticed. In his formal report, he recounted his own experiences in flat, declarative tones. "Among the lost," he wrote, "was my wife." As to the future. "I believe that a sea wall, which would have broken the swells, would have saved much loss of both life and property." Cora's body was found a few weeks later, identified by her engagement ring.

Over the next decade, a seawall was finally built and most of the city's grade was raised. Hurricanes have continued to pound Galveston every now and then but without the disastrous losses of the 1900 storm. That dreadful catastrophe reminds us of the folly of underestimating the power of nature, even in the most modern of circumstances. Its upshot also suggests the stubborn resilience of human will in the face of calamity.

On Sunday morning following the storm, a baker named Bernard La Coume had opened his door and discovered a barrel on the front porch. His son, Clarence, later told the story many times to his granddaughter, Linda Macdonald, who lives in Galveston today and relates the anecdote with relish. Bernard tapped the barrel and found that it was filled with wine. "Don't ever forget," he told Clarence, "that even in times such as these, the Good Lord remembers the needs of a Frenchman."

# Surviving Camille

## By Lyle Prescott

*The author of the following narrative, Lyle Prescott, was fifteen when Hurricane Camille hit the Mississippi Gulf Coast on August 17, 1969. With wind speeds as high as 210 miles per hour, Camille may have been the most powerful hurricane to ever strike North America. Prescott was visiting her relatives in a coastal Mississippi town when the storm made landfall. Surging water quickly destroyed the first floor of their house, and the family had to climb out of a second-story window onto a neighbor's garage roof to keep from drowning. Prescott now works as an editor for* Ranger Rick, *a monthly magazine published by the National Wildlife Federation.*

I couldn't believe my eyes. It was just before midnight, and a crashing sound by the front door made me look over that way. The ocean had knocked down the door and was gushing into the living room.

It was August 17, 1969. I was 15, and I was visiting my Aunt Rusty, Uncle John, and eight-year-old cousin Charlie in Long Beach, Mississippi. For two days, we had been preparing for Hurricane Camille, which was headed our way. Lots of people were fleeing the area, but my aunt thought we'd be OK if we stayed. She'd grown up there and had been in other hurricanes—including the one in 1946 when the tree in her front yard blew down.

From the front of the house, we had a clear view of the Gulf of Mexico. It was about a football-field's length away across a wide beach. Uncle John knew that if the water rose more than 15 feet (4.5 m), it would bang against the house. So he'd nailed heavy boards across the front door and windows. But when the hurricane hit, nothing could stop it.

Earlier that day, I had wandered into the kitchen. Aunt Rusty was at the sink filling pots (in case the water got cut off), and Uncle John was loading batteries into flashlights (in case the

electricity got cut off). "Exactly how does a hurricane work?" I
had asked them. When neither one could give me a good answer, I went to the bookshelf and came back with the "H"
encyclopedia.

"A hurricane," I read out loud, "is a whirling storm with
winds stronger than 74 miles per hour. The winds swirl around
the eye, a calm area in the center of the storm." I studied a drawing of a hurricane. It looked like a white doughnut with a small
hole in the middle.

## Everything Began to Change Fast

That night, it had begun to rain around 9 o'clock. By 10, the
electricity had gone off. And by 11, the wind was roaring like
crazy.

We were huddled on the couch. I was excited but not scared.
What was there to be scared of? The house was 100 years old,
and it hadn't been knocked down by a storm yet.

That was before the front door burst open and everything began to change fast.

When the water started surging into the living room, we just
stood there in shock. Then my aunt and my cousin and I scam-
pered partway up the stairs leading to the second floor, with my
uncle not far behind.

I turned around to watch what was happening below. Churn-
ing water swept up furniture and banged it against the walls.
This'll be a total mess to clean up in the morning, I remember
thinking.

I watched the couch plow into the wall, leaving a big, ragged
hole. The water kept rising. We moved to the top of the steps. I
looked down and saw another surge of water knock the couch
through the wall and into the kitchen. The downstairs walls were
being smashed to bits. Pretty soon the second story was floating
like a boat.

A feeling of panic flittered in my stomach. We could get
smashed up too, I thought. Or we might drown. But death was
for old people! How could this be happening? I felt sick. A loud
creaking sound from above made me look up. The wind was
blowing so hard that it made the ceiling shift back and forth.

"Are we going to die?" I blurted out. I didn't really want to
hear the truth—I knew we might. I just wanted to hear someone say "NO!"—in a clear, sure voice.

"I don't know," my uncle said. "Does anyone have a cigarette?" I felt like strangling him. By now I was feeling really sick.

## Getting the Adults to Understand

A few minutes later we stood by the second-story back window in the hall. The first floor was gone. Water was everywhere. The ceiling was groaning, and I thought it might fall on us.

All I wanted to do was get outside. Maybe we'd drown out there. But outside was coming inside fast, so at this point we might drown inside too. At least outside we wouldn't get clobbered by a falling ceiling.

"We'll wait for the eye of the storm before we go outside," Aunt Rusty said. "Then we'll swim inland."

I didn't want to wait. I was terrified inside this wobbly box-of-a-house. I had been frustrated before when grownups didn't seem to listen to me. But it had never mattered so much. Somehow I had to get my aunt and uncle to understand. I remembered the diagram in the encyclopedia.

"Listen," I said, "it's possible the eye could miss us completely." I made a circle with my thumb and index finger. Then I ran my

*With winds in excess of two hundred miles per hour and tides over twenty feet, Hurricane Camille smashed into the Mississippi Gulf Coast in August 1969.*

other index finger across the edge of the circle to show how the eye could miss us.

The ceiling made a grunting sound and rippled like a bedsheet in the wind. Looking out the window, we could see that our second-story "boat" had sailed along and was now lodged near the big oak tree in the backyard.

"Maybe that's right—maybe we're not going to get the eye," my uncle said to my aunt. They talked about it for what seemed like an hour but was probably a minute. Then my aunt said, "OK, we'll go out the window."

## A Feeling of Wild Hope

Hallelujah! In two seconds, I slipped out the window into the water and swam a few feet away. The wind was howling like a thousand animals, but the water was surprisingly calm. I couldn't tell how deep it was, but my feet didn't touch the ground. I grabbed hold of the tree and held on tight. Just then my sandal caught on something and slipped off my foot. I should dive down and get it, I thought. My mother would want me to have shoes on in a hurricane. I stared down into the dark water and came to my senses. It would be just plain stupid to dive under this dangerous water!

When my aunt shone a flashlight out at me, I smiled to let them know I was OK. A minute later she climbed out, clutching my cousin tightly to her. Then, just as my uncle stepped out, the roof collapsed behind him.

We climbed through the tree and grabbed onto the neighbor's garage roof as it floated by. For the rest of the night, we huddled in the middle of the roof. For a while I thought we were moving along so fast that we would end up in Texas. But whenever I shone the flashlight around, I kept seeing the same pink nightgown hanging in the same tree. The garage roof somehow must have gotten stuck and we weren't moving at all! I guess it was the roar of the wind and the sloshing of the water that made it seem as if we were moving.

Rain poured down on us. I was drenched and cold to the bone. But a feeling of wild hope was rising in me—maybe we were actually going to survive! I remember thinking that if I lived to see sunlight, I would never, ever complain about anything again.

Dawn finally lit the sky. The rain had stopped. The ocean had crept back to where it usually was. And we had survived! Later we would learn that many others had not been so lucky.

I looked around and could see that we were in a backyard about half a block inland from where we had started. In both directions as far as we could see, all the houses in the row closest to the beach were gone.

We stumbled off the roof and climbed over the broken chairs, refrigerators, clothes, books, cameras, and torn-up board until we got back to where the house had been. The only thing left of it was the concrete front step.

I have to be honest—in the many years since then, I have complained at least once or twice. But I've never forgotten the lessons I learned that night—about the power of nature, and how fantastic it is to be alive!

# Hunting Hugo

## By Jeffrey M. Masters

*The following selection is by Jeffrey M. Masters, a meteorologist who formerly worked as a flight director on one of the National Oceanic and Atmospheric Administration's "hurricane hunter" aircraft. Masters describes the experience of flying into Hurricane Hugo, a category 5 storm that swept through the Bahamas and eventually hit South Carolina on September 21, 1989. Hugo turned out to be stronger than Masters had expected, and the plane lost power in one engine and came close to crashing as it traversed the violent winds of the hurricane's eye wall. The flight crew had to seek assistance from a nearby Air Force reconnaissance plane, which guided the damaged aircraft back out of Hugo's eye. Later analysis revealed that the plane had hit a tornadolike vortex embedded in the eye wall; it had also sustained turbulence stronger than five times the force of gravity.*

As I look out my window, the ocean grows closer. Powerful wind gusts of 40 to 50 m.p.h. drive crescent-shaped white-capped waves over the ocean surface. We cross over several hurricane feeder bands—tall heaps of piled cumulus clouds arranged in picturesque lines that spiral into the eyewall. Ahead, the first major spiral band—an ominous dark mass of forbidding cumulonimbus clouds—blocks our path.

It's September 1989, and I'm aboard one of the National Oceanic and Atmospheric Administration's P-3 Orion "Hurricane Hunter" aircraft—the NOAA 42, affectionately called "the Princess."

NOAA 42 is part of a two-aircraft research mission out of Barbados, heading for the newly formed Hurricane Hugo. Our aircraft will repeatedly penetrate the eye at the lowest safe altitude and gather detailed information on the low-level storm environment and air-sea interaction. Our sister aircraft, the high-altitude NOAA 43, will fly at 20,000 feet and circle the periphery

Jeffrey M. Masters, "Hunting Hugo," *Weatherwise*, vol. 52, September 1999, p. 20. Copyright © 1999 by Heldref Publications, 1319 18th Street NW, Washington, DC 20036-1802. Reproduced by permission.

of the storm and study the hurricane's large-scale environment. No Hurricane Hunter aircraft have yet penetrated the storm.

## Pushing the Limits

In order to get to the eye, we must fly directly through the hurricane's strongest winds and most violent turbulence—the dangerous eyewall. Today, we are pushing the limits of safe hurricane flying by going into the eyewall at 1,500 feet, the altitude where the hurricane's winds and turbulence are at their worst.

There are 16 people on board: three flight crew members in the cockpit, one navigator, one radio operator, three electronics engineers, six scientists, a newspaper reporter, and myself. It is my job as flight director to ensure the safety of the mission from a meteorological perspective, and call for a climb to a higher, safer altitude if I judge the storm is too dangerous.

"OK, leveling out at 1,500 feet," calls out aircraft commander Lowell Genzlinger from the cockpit. "How does this track look?" I study the radar display and wind readings and respond, "Let's hold this track through this spiral band, and see what things look like when we pop out on the other side."

"OK, sounds good," he replies. "We're getting pretty close now, time to button things up."

"Set condition one!" Lowell's voice crackles over the aircraft's loudspeakers and intercom. When announced by the aircraft commander, "condition one" requires all hands to return to their seats and prepare for turbulence. Throughout the airplane, the crew stashes away flight bags, clipboards, and other loose items that could turn into dangerous missiles in severe turbulence. I buckle my seat belt, but don't bother with the shoulder harness. The turbulence in a spiral band is never too bad.

Twilight falls. Thick gray clouds engulf us. The winds jump to 85 m.p.h. Minor turbulent wind gusts bounce and bump the aircraft, and a new sound joins the ever-present roar of the engines—the clatter of heavy rain lashing the fuselage.

Two minutes later, the sky lightens and the turbulence suddenly stops. We emerge from the spiral band into the clear. A typical spiral band penetration, no big deal. The wind has dropped to 50 m.p.h., with a slight shift in direction. Good. With a wind this low between the spiral band and eyewall, it is unlikely that Hugo is more than a Category-3 storm.

I adjust my radar display to zoom in on the eye, now only 10

minutes away. The bright oranges and reds of the eyewall lie before us, growing closer and more ominous with each sweep of
the radar. The eyewall looks impenetrable, now just seven minutes away. I suppress an urge to chicken out and order a climb to
5,000 feet. The intercom is silent, but I feel the unspoken tension
of the crew. I wait for either Lowell or lead scientist Frank Marks
to order a climb to 5,000 feet. Neither of them do.

Three minutes from the eyewall, I check my wind readings.
Winds are well below hurricane force—a mere 60 m.p.h. This is
remarkably low, so close to the eyewall. Hugo may not even be a
Category-3 storm! I make my final decision not to order a climb
to 5,000 feet. We're going in at 1,500! I look out my window at
the approaching eyewall, a tall dark wall of forbidding thunderstorm clouds.

## Into the Eyewall

We hit the eyewall. Darkness falls. Powerful gusts of wind and
torrential rains hammer the airplane. My stomach is clenched into
a tight knot. The ride is choppy and uncomfortable.

I grab the computer console with both hands, trying to steady
my vision on the blurred computer readouts. I don't like what I
see. The winds are rising too quickly, the pressure falling too fast.
Hugo is far more powerful than expected. The aircraft lurches
and bucks.

Thirty seconds in, a minute-and-a-half to go. The turbulence
grows worse, second only to the incredible turbulence we encountered in Hurricane Emily in 1987 as it made landfall on the
mountains of Hispaniola. During that flight, we hit the highest
G forces ever encountered by our P-3's in a hurricane—three
G's—and had to abort the flight when the extreme turbulence
caused a dangerous vibration in the wings.

Hugo is stronger than Emily. I am very concerned. We should
not be at 1,500 feet!

I fumble for the intercom switch, find it. "Winds are 135
m.p.h., surface pressure 960 millibars," I say. "Hugo's at least a
Category-4."

Frank breaks in. "Lowell, Jeff, this ride is way too rough! Let's
climb to 5,000 when we finish this penetration."

"Roger!" is Lowell's terse reply. Both he and copilot Gerry
McKim must wrestle with the controls of the airplane. The turbulence is so violent that one pilot alone cannot stay in control.

There is no possibility of climbing now; the pilots need the full power of the engines just to keep the airplane flying straight and level.

One minute in, one minute to go. The intercom goes silent as everyone hangs on and the pilots concentrate on getting us through the eyewall. Gerry does a great job fighting off the turbulence and keeping the airplane on track. Winds are now 155 m.p.h., still rising. Pressure 955 millibars, dropping fast. Hugo is almost a Category-5 hurricane.

A fierce updraft wrenches the airplane, slams us into our seats with twice the force of gravity. Seconds later, we dangle weightless as a stomach-wrenching downdraft slams us downward.

Another updraft, much stronger, grabs the aircraft. I regret forgetting to fasten my shoulder harness, as I struggle to keep from bashing into the computer console. Seconds later, a huge downdraft blasts us, hurling the loosened gear against walls and floor. Gerry and Lowell are barely in control of the aircraft.

Grimly, I hang on to my console against the violent turbulence and watch the numbers. A 20 m.p.h. updraft. A 22 m.p.h. downdraft. Sustained winds now 185 m.p.h., gusting to 196 m.p.h. Pressure plummeting, down to 930 millibars. Hugo is a Category-5 hurricane, and we are in the eyewall at 1,500 feet! One strong downdraft has the power to send us plunging into the ocean. We have no options other than to gut it out and make it to the eye, where we can climb to a safer altitude.

A minute-and-a-half gone, half-a-minute to go. A colossal 45 m.p.h. updraft seizes the airplane. A shower of loose gear flies through the cabin as the airplane lurches violently. Gerry fights the updraft off, keeps the airplane level and headed towards the eye. We're almost there!

"Looks like it's lightening up out there!" Lowell's relieved voice breaks the intense silence. Sure enough, the sky lightens, the clouds thin, the rain abates. We are at the edge of the eyewall. A big smile of jubilation erases my anxious frown. We got away with a penetration at 1,500 feet in a Category-5 storm!

## Disaster

Then, disaster. Thick, dark clouds suddenly envelop the aircraft. A titanic fist of wind, three times the force of gravity, smashes us. I am thrown into the computer console, bounce off, and for one terrifying instant find myself looking down at a precipitous angle

*A NOAA P-3 flies in the eye of a hurricane. Known as "hurricane hunters," the aircraft help predict hurricane intensity and landfall.*

at navigator Sean White across the aisle from me. A second massive jolt rocks the aircraft. Gear and debris—from tools and computers to soda cans and briefcases—that had been loosened by the previous turbulence flies about the aircraft, bouncing off walls, ceiling, and crewmembers.

A third terrific blow, almost six times the force of gravity, staggers the airplane. Clip boards, flight bags, and headsets sail past my head as I am hurled into the console. Terrible thundering crashing sounds boom through the cabin: I hear crew members crying out. I scream inwardly. "This is what it feels like to die in battle," I think. We are going down. The final moments of the five Hurricane Hunter missions that never returned must have been like this.

The aircraft lurches out of control into a hard right bank. We plunge towards the ocean, our number three engine in flames. Debris hangs from the number four engine.

The turbulence suddenly stops. The clouds part. The darkness lifts. We fall into the eye of Hurricane Hugo.

"We've got fire coming out of number three!" electrical engineer Terry Schricker's urgent cry shatters the stunned silence on the intercom.

"And I see something hanging from number four," adds Sean, his voice sounding strangely calm.

For several eternal terrifying seconds, I watch the massive, white-frothed waves below us grow huge and close. I wait for impact, praying for survival. With two engines damaged, both on the same wing, I know that our odds are not good.

But my prayers are answered by the cool, professional reaction of the cockpit crew. Gerry snaps us up out of the right-rolling dive just 880 feet from the water. Flight engineer Steve Wade hits the kill switch on engine number three, and the 30-foot long flames shooting out of it die as the flow of fuel chokes off. Lowell and Frank take charge of keeping us in the eye, scanning the inside to size up where our path should take us.

A dark mass of clouds lies directly ahead, seconds away. Is it the eyewall? Or merely harmless low scud in the eye? There is no time [to] think, no time to plan the best flight path. We must turn now to avoid the clouds. If we hit the eyewall again at this altitude, the storm will surely kill us. We must stay in the eye.

## The Wrong Choice

"It's clear to the right!" Lowell shouts out. Immediately, Gerry throws us into a hard right roll. I look at my radar display, and quickly compute our position. A right turn is the wrong choice! We popped into the eye off-center, on its right side, and now must trace out an almost impossibly tight four-mile diameter circle to stay in the eye. The dark clouds that Gerry turned us from were merely harmless low level scud in the eye. We should have turned left! It is too late to call for a course change, though. We are committed to this turn.

Tense seconds pass. I watch the wind speed indicator as the winds slowly increase: 30 m.p.h., 40 m.p.h., 50 m.p.h. The eyewall grows closer, a huge ominous wall of seething dark clouds spinning past my window. Gerry has us banked over as far as he dares, at a 30° angle. The airplane cannot sustain a tighter turn without its number three engine.

I can see only a blurred, white wall of clouds, frighteningly close, out my window. I lean out into the aisle to see the same view out the cockpit window. I see Frank standing up, craning his head towards the right upper window, straining to see where

we are headed. "Keep on coming!" I hear him call out to the pilots. The left wingtip is now just a few hundred feet from the
eyewall.

A fist of clouds protrudes out from the eyewall, blocking our
path. We penetrate. Turbulence rocks the aircraft. The winds
jump to 75 m.p.h. We are in the eyewall again. Gerry banks us
even harder right, a 35° roll. We are dangerously close to stalling.
An eternal few seconds later, we emerge into the eye again.

"Keep on coming!" I hear Frank say, once again. Again, eyewall clouds grab at the airplane, shaking us with frightening turbulence. Another eternity later, we pop out in the clear as Gerry
maneuvers us out of the clouds, keeping us barely within the eye.
We are now fast approaching the deadly part of the eyewall
where we originally entered the eye. Our turn is nearly complete.

"That's it, you've got it!" I hear Frank exclaim.

Gerry relaxes the steep bank, and heads us into the center of
the eye. A few seconds later, he puts us into a left roll that will
keep us comfortably in the eye for as long as we want to circle.
He brings the nose of the aircraft up, and we begin a steady spiraling climb. The immediate danger is past.

## Awesome, Terrifying, and Supernatural

I look out my window, and behold the eye of Hurricane Hugo
in its full fury. It is awesome, terrifying, and supernatural. The eyewall, a towering prison of blinding-white, boiling, virulent
clouds, rings us on all sides. We are so low that I can see beneath
the ragged bottom edge of the eyewall clouds, where Hugo's 160
m.p.h. surface winds whip the ocean into a chaotic frenzy of col-
liding 50-foot-high waves.

I watch with fascinated dread as white masses of tortured
clouds bulge in and out along the eyewall. I angrily curse myself
for failing my primary duty, ensuring the safety of the mission
from a meteorological perspective. My job today is done. It is now
up to Gerry and Lowell [to get] us out of the crisis I got us into.

Lowell's voice comes on the intercom: "OK, we're going to
circle in the eye as long as we can and climb to our maximum altitude before we attempt to punch out through the eyewall . . .
Number three engine is shut down, and it looks like we got the
fire fully extinguished. Can anyone back there take a good look
at number four and tell us what it looks like?"

Across the aisle from me, Sean looks out his window and responds, "It looks like it might have a dislodged de-icing boot."

"Well, let's hope it doesn't tear off and get caught in the propeller," says Lowell. "We need to lighten the plane up as much as possible to gain altitude, so we'll be dumping fuel. I'll want all communications equipment and electrical gear that could cause a spark powered off."

The commander of NOAA 43 contacts us, and we tell him what happened. He will advise the Air Force airplane of our situation.

I step into the cockpit to confer with Lowell. Scientist Pete Black is there, too.

"So what's the plan, Lowell?" I ask.

"We've got to stay in the eye and lighten the aircraft up as much as possible," Lowell responds. He sounds very worried, but is focused, in command. I look across the cockpit at Gerry. He is concentrating intensely on flying, keeping the airplane safely within the eye and steadily climbing. Between Lowell and Gerry, the flight engineer intently eyes the engine gauges, and keeps a particularly close eye on the engine four's temperature gauge, which hovers near the red zone.

"The cockpit G-meter shows we took five and half G's up and three and half G's down," continues Lowell, now sounding really concerned. "The P-3 is only rated to plus three and minus two G's, so we may have some serious structural damage. We'll have to climb as high as we can and find a part of the eyewall to exit through with a minimum of turbulence."

"Five and half G's!" I exclaim. No Hurricane Hunter aircraft has ever taken more than three G's. We are lucky to be alive.

"Lowell, we're ready back here for fuel dumping," says electrical engineer Alan Goldstein over the intercom. "Everything is powered down."

"Roger, we'll begin dumping now," replies Lowell. It will take about 15 minutes to dump 15,000 of our 50,000 pounds of fuel.

I walk to the back of the aircraft. I take one look down the aisle, and gawk in amazement. The inside of the airplane is trashed. Scientist Jim McFadden is there, organizing clean up efforts.

"So no one back here got hurt?" I ask him. As I look in his eyes I see my thoughts and fears mirrored. We both know these may be our last minutes left to live.

He shakes his head, "No, and it's a damn miracle, too. Look at the life raft!" I look to where he motions. Sitting in the center of the aisle is our 200-pound life raft. Jim points to a one-inch dent in the inch-thick steel handrail that runs the length of the ceiling. "The raft hit the ceiling so hard, it put that dent in the handrail. We're lucky no one got killed by the thing!"

I survey the scene of destruction with awe and dismay. The galley is piled knee-high with an amazing collection of trash, food, utensils, and other gear. The contents of our toilet grace the floor. Alan stands there, surveying the mess.

"Who had the honor of sitting back here?" I ask him. "I did," he answers gloomily. "The locks failed on all of the drawers back here. It was all I could do to fend off all the soda cans that came flying out of the cooler at me."

## Deadly Scenarios

I help Jim, Alan, and other crew members pick up the debris and strap things down. As we work, we talk about the incredible turbulence we just survived. We talk about the damage to the engines. We don't talk about our odds of survival. When I look anyone in the eye, I see the same sick fear, the same sort of deadly scenarios playing through their minds that are playing through mine: We penetrate the eyewall. Another engine fails. We ditch into the raging seas below. We deploy our life raft, and die one by one as Hugo's 50-foot waves and 160 m.p.h. winds capsize our boat and send us to a watery doom.

I return to my seat and look out at the fearsome eyewall of Hugo again. I feel trapped and helpless. To cheer myself up, I snap a series of photographs of the eyewall, hoping that someday I will be able to use them to relate the incredible story of the near-disastrous first encounter with Hurricane Hugo.

I hear Gerry's voice over the intercom. "Okay, we're all done dumping fuel. You can turn back on any equipment you turned off."

Terry and Alan turn the communications equipment back on, and Lowell immediately contacts TEAL 57, the Air Force C-130 reconnaissance airplane sent into the storm by the National Hurricane Center to provide information on Hugo's position and intensity.

"NOAA 42, this is TEAL 57," radios the voice of Lieutenant Commander Terry Self, aircraft commander of TEAL 57, and veteran of 10 years of hurricane flying. "NOAA 43 has advised us of your situation. Can you give us your position and altitude, and update us on your status?"

"Roger," relies Lowell. "We are circling the eye in a left orbit at 5,000 feet. We've lost the number three engine, and have damage to the number four engine. We'd like you to come fly by and take a look at our number four engine, and inspect us for any other damage we can't see."

"Sure thing, NOAA 42," says Self. "We'll penetrate the west eyewall and come down and have a look at you. TEAL 57 out."

"Ten-four. Thanks, TEAL 57! NOAA 42 out."

We wait anxiously for the Air Force airplane to penetrate the eyewall. They are definitely sticking their necks out for us—I have never heard of an Air Force airplane penetrating an intense hurricane at an altitude less than 10,000 feet. Only NOAA airplanes risk going in hurricanes at altitudes below 10,000 feet! Finally, the radio crackles back to life with the voice of Commander Self.

"NOAA 42, we are in the eye. We got a terrific pounding going through the west eyewall coming in, but are still in one piece!" My heart sinks at this news. What chance did we have of making it through the eyewall with only three engines?

The TEAL 57 performs two difficult fly-bys above and below our plane. They report no obvious damage, other than the dislodged de-icing boot hanging from engine four.

Commander Self radios us, "We're going to exit the eye now through the east eyewall and see how rough it is for you over there. We'll continue penetrating the eyewall until we find a soft spot for you."

"Roger TEAL 57, that'd be greatly appreciated!" replies Lowell.

I say a silent thank you to the brave crew of TEAL 57. The extreme turbulence in Hugo's eyewall almost killed us, but they are willing to risk it several times so we may find safe passage.

"Better not try the east eyewall!" Self ruefully informs us, after they finish their penetration. "We'll circle around to the south now, and come into the eye through the south eyewall." Gerry keeps us circling the eye, but has now pushed us as high as our three engines will take us. We are at 7,000 feet. Any further attempts to climb bring the temperature needle on the overtaxed number four engine into the dangerous red zone. We must exit Hugo's eye at 7,000 feet.

I glance at Janice Griffith, the newspaper reporter from Barbados. I meet her wide-eyed, alarmed gaze, and think I should smile to reassure her, but don't have it in me. She is probably the least frightened among us. For all she knows, this situation is routine on hurricane flights! I return to my seat to wait for the next penetration of TEAL 57.

A few minutes later, the intercom crackles to life again with the voice of Commander Self, who informs us that the south eyewall is just as bad as the east eyewall. They will now try to find a soft spot in the northeast eyewall.

We will have to leave the eye in just a few more minutes, regardless of whether the Air Force airplane can find a soft spot. I wait. We have been in the eye of Hugo for almost an hour.

## A Way Out

Finally, the intercom comes to life again.

"NOAA 42, this is TEAL 57. We have just penetrated the northeast eyewall, and it wasn't too bad! You might want to give it a try. If you look on your radar display, you should be able to see where a weakness has developed in the northeast eyewall."

I look over at my radar display. Sure enough, an area of weaker echoes has developed in a narrow section of the northeast eyewall. If we can hit the soft spot just right, the ride might not be too rough. Gerry's voice, terse and determined, comes in over the intercom:

"Okay, we're going to follow the Air Force airplane out now. Make sure all gear is stowed away. One minute to penetration. Set condition one!"

The klaxon sounds overhead, warning of upcoming turbulence. The big plane suddenly rolls out of its steep turn and levels out, headed for the northeast eyewall. The huge, imposing wall of clouds rushes towards us at high speed. I buckle my shoulder harness and hang on to the table with both hands.

We hit the eyewall. Darkness falls. Intense blasts of turbulent wind rock the airplane. Torrential rain hammers the fuselage. The winds shoot up to 170 m.p.h., gusting to 190. The three remaining engines whine and roar as Gerry fights off a powerful updraft. The turbulence is rough, but survivable. We cross the inner eyewall without hitting any incredible jolts like those that nearly knocked us from the sky on our way in.

Half-a-minute gone, one minute to go. The turbulence lessens. The updrafts and down-drafts diminish, the winds drop to 150 m.p.h. We are definitely in a weak region of the eyewall! The radar display shows yellows and greens surrounding us, where before there were only the strongest reds and oranges.

One minute gone, half-a-minute to go. The airplane is barely shaking now, the turbulence is so light. It is hard to believe we are in the eyewall of Hugo! The big plane lumbers on towards the edge of the eyewall.

Finally, sunshine! We made it! The sullen dark clouds of the eyewall slip away, and the sun shines down at us through a thin veil of high cirrus clouds. A huge smile of jubilation replaces my worried frown.

Praise God! The sun never looked so good. I can hear cheers ringing out from the crew in the cabin behind me.

"Nice flying, Gerry!" I call out over the intercom.

"That wasn't too bad," Gerry replies, matter-of-factly.

Lowell contacts the Air Force airplane and gives them the good news.

Now well clear of the eyewall, we turn and head for Barbados, an hour-and-a-half away. NOAA 43 appears out the right window, hovering protectively over us. The sight of our sister aircraft feels very reassuring.

I unbuckle my seat belt and shoulder harness, and head back to the galley. Most of the crew are gathering there, trading stories on what we've just been through.

"What happened to [engine] number three?" wonders scientist Hugh Willoughby.

"It exploded!" Terry exclaims. "Flames were shooting 30 feet aft of the airplane. I swear I could feel the heat of the fire through the wall!"

"You probably did!" I remark. "That thing puts out a lot of heat!"

Terry looks at me with dark, frightened eyes. "I'm all done flying," He says emphatically. "At least, flying into hurricanes. This is my last flight!"

I look at him and think to myself, "Amen, brother!"

# Epilogue

Hurricane Hugo smashed through the Caribbean and southeastern U.S. with incredible fury over the next week, killing hundreds and causing over $9 billion in damage—the most destructive hurricane in history, at the time. Most of the crew of NOAA

42 flew in Hugo again, on our undamaged sister aircraft. But for me, the nearly disastrous first penetration of Hugo's eye was my last flight. I quit the Hurricane Hunters a few months later.

NOAA 42 spent a month on Barbados undergoing a thorough check of its structural integrity before it was cleared to fly back to Florida, where it received a three-month long maintenance overhaul. No hurricane-related damage to the aircraft was found, except for the missing de-icing boot on the engine four and a failed fuel control sensor on the engine three.

The instrument that recorded the amazing G-forces was found to be accurate, and engineers analyzing the data could only conclude that luck and the toughness of the P-3 airplane saved us from destruction. The aircraft continues to fly into hurricanes to this day.

Later analysis of the data taken during our amazing flight into Hugo revealed that we hit a tornado-like vortex embedded in the eyewall when the hurricane was at its peak intensity. These eyewall vortices had been suspected but never before observed, and ongoing research suggests that similar vortices may be responsible for some of the incredible damage hurricanes can inflict when they strike land. When the next mighty hurricane threatens our coast, the Hurricane Hunters will be in the storm to learn more. Say a prayer for them.

# Preventing Calamity

# Improving
# Hurricane
# Forecasting

## BY RICHARD A. KERR

*Improved observational technology and computer modeling are enhancing meteorologists' ability to forecast where hurricanes will hit, explains Richard A. Kerr in the following selection. Dropwindsondes—instrument packages that are released into hurricanes to record data—are now equipped with Global Positioning System satellite technology, resulting in more accurate wind mapping. Moreover, new computer models allow scientists to examine hurricanes in finer detail, which greatly improves storm-track predictions, reports Kerr. Kerr is a news writer for* Science, *a weekly journal.*

Hurricane forecasting has come a long way since one sneaked up unannounced on Galveston Island, Texas, in 1900 and killed 8000 people. Nowadays, meteorologists know when a storm is on its way, but predicting just where it will hit land still isn't easy. For most of the past half-century, forecasters have struggled to narrow their predictions of a hurricane's next move, but as recently as the 1970s, guesses of a hurricane's position 24 hours ahead of time were off by an average of more than 200 kilometers. Now hurricane researchers finally have something to celebrate.

"It's been a pretty exciting 5 years," says hurricane specialist Russell Elsberry of the Naval Postgraduate School in Monterey, California. Better observations of the streams of winds that carry hurricanes toward land are feeding new computer models for predicting how those winds will shift. And, as recent analyses—

Richard A. Kerr, "Forecasters Learning to Read a Hurricane's Mind," *Science*, vol. 284, April 23, 1999, p. 563. Copyright © 1999 by the American Association for the Advancement of Science. Reproduced by permission.

including one in [the March 1999] *Bulletin of the American Mete-orological Society*—show, these new tools are getting results. "It's quite clear that the [U.S] National Hurricane Center has been making much improved track forecasts" of future storm move-ment, says Elsberry. The new forecasting skill means that crowded coasts will have more time to prepare for storms, and warnings can be limited to smaller sections of coast, saving millions of dol-lars on unnecessary evacuations.

# New Observational Techniques

Hurricane forecasting has spent a long time in the doldrums. In the 35 years after record keeping was begun in 1954, forecasts of a storm's position 24 hours in the future improved by only about 1 kilometer per year, even after satellite images made it easier to track the position, winds, and extent of a hurricane. One prob-lem was that neither satellite images nor the scattered data from weather buoys and ships offered many clues about the stream of air surrounding a storm, which determines its speed and direc-tion.

"There is no substitute for in situ observations," says meteo-rologist Kerry Emanuel of the Massachusetts Institute of Tech-nology. For 15 years, researchers had been collecting those ob-servations by flying aircraft near the storms and releasing instrumented packages called dropwindsondes—a sort of weather balloon in reverse that radios back wind speed and direction, temperature, pressure, and humidity as it falls. But those efforts were sporadic until 1997, when the National Weather Service (NWS) made such observations routine and introduced a new dropwindsonde that tracks itself using the satellite-based Global Positioning System, allowing more precise wind mapping. The NWS also acquired a Gulfstream-IV jet, which could fly higher and faster around storms than the traditional hurricane-hunter aircraft, probing more of the nearby atmosphere.

In the March [1999] *Bulletin of the American Meteorological So-ciety*, Sim Aberson and James Franklin of the National Oceanic and Atmospheric Administration's (NOAA's) Hurricane Re-search Division in Miami, Florida, describe the payoff: The 1997 dropwindsonde observations improved storm-track forecasts by 31% 24 hours ahead, by 32% at 36 hours, and by 12% at 48 hours, they report, compared to computer forecasts made with-out the observations. The tropics were relatively quiet in 1997, prompting just five missions by the Gulfstream-IV, so "you don't want to make too much of the numbers," says Franklin. . . .

## Computer Modeling

Along with better data, forecasters have better tools for inter-preting the information. Their primary aid is computer model-ing that incorporates the latest observations to create a picture of the storm and its surroundings and calculates how the storm will move and develop. "There has been a quantum increase in the skill of the models," says Stephen Lord, a deputy director at the NWS's National Centers for Environmental Prediction in Camp Springs, Maryland.

The prime example has been the hurricane model developed by Yoshio Kurihara, Morris Bender, and Robert Tuleya of NOAA's Geophysical Fluid Dynamics Laboratory (GFDL) in Princeton, New Jersey. The GFDL model works on two scales. Like standard global atmospheric models, it simulates the atmo-sphere in broad strokes to capture the river of air, thousands of kilometers across, that sets the hurricane's overall course. But it also zooms in on the hurricane's vortex, using the latest satellite and in situ data to model the storm and the way it interacts with its surroundings in fine detail.

In tests prior to becoming operational at the National Hurri-cane Center (NHC) in 1995, the GFDL model outperformed its predecessor, logging average track errors that were about 12%, 24%, and 28% better at 24, 48, and 72 hours, respectively. Since then, "it's been the best performer" of the half-dozen models that NHC forecasters consult before issuing an official forecast, ac-cording to James Gross of the NHC.

## Accelerating Improvement

Even so, it can be hard to tell whether better data and models are actually improving the official forecasts, because the improved tools are new and forecasters have always had good seasons and bad, depending on the nature of the storms. But meteorologist Colin McAdie of the NHC thinks track forecasts are improving at an accelerating pace. His recent analysis shows that at all fore-cast times, the predictions improved twice as fast during 1992 to '96, the period when the GFDL model debuted, as they had dur-ing the previous 2 decades. The routine dropwindsonde observa-tions that began in 1997 seem to have helped sustain that progress.

Such improvements should allow the NWS to target its hurricane warnings more precisely. When the weather service issues a hurricane warning, prompting an evacuation, it generally includes a stretch of coast three times longer than the section that eventually suffers high winds, just to be sure—which means that hundreds of kilometers are cleared but suffer little damage. With costs averaging half a million dollars per kilometer of evacuated coast, according to the NWS, not to mention a toll in public goodwill, that's an expensive insurance policy. If the improvements of the '90s can be continued, averting hurricane disasters should be cheaper and less disruptive.

# A Guide to Hurricane Preparedness

BY THE NATIONAL OCEANIC AND
ATMOSPHERIC ADMINISTRATION

*The National Oceanic and Atmospheric Administration (NOAA),
part of the U.S. Department of Commerce, strives to improve hurricane
forecasting and diminish the threat of these powerful storms to life and
property. The National Weather Service (NWS), an arm of the NOAA,
issues hurricane watches and warnings and educates community leaders
and the public in disaster preparedness. This selection reveals why U.S.
populations are increasingly vulnerable to hurricanes and provides helpful
advice about what individuals and families can do when a hurricane
threatens their community. It offers specific suggestions about hurricane
preparedness, such as learning the location of shelters and storing nonper-
ishable food and water, as well as giving advice on what people should do
during and after the storm, such as finding refuge in an interior hallway
and avoiding the use of candles. The NOAA advises all families living
in hurricane-prone areas to develop a disaster plan so that all family
members know how to respond when asked to evacuate or take shelter.*

A hurricane is a type of tropical cyclone, the general term
for all circulating weather systems over tropical waters
(counterclockwise in the Northern Hemisphere). Tropical cyclones are classified as follows:

- *Tropical depression:* An organized system of clouds and thunderstorms with a defined circulation and maximum sustained winds of 38 mph (33 knots) or less.
- *Tropical storm:* An organized system of strong thunderstorms

National Oceanic and Atmospheric Administration, "Hurricanes . . . Unleashing
Nature's Fury: A Preparedness Guide," www.nws.noaa.gov, March 1994.

with a defined circulation and maximum sustained winds of
39 to 73 mph (34–63 knots).
- *Hurricane:* An intense tropical weather system with a well
defined circulation and maximum sustained winds of 74
mph (64 knots) or higher. In the western Pacific, hurricanes
are called "typhoons," and similar storms in the Indian
Ocean are called "cyclones."

Hurricanes are products of a tropical ocean and atmosphere.
Powered by heat from the sea, they are steered by the easterly trade
winds and the temperate westerlies as well as by their own fero-
cious energy. Around their core, winds grow with great velocity,
generating violent seas. Moving ashore, they sweep the ocean inward while spawning tornadoes and producing torrential rains and
floods. Each year, on average, 10 tropical storms, of which six become hurricanes, develop over the Atlantic Ocean, Caribbean Sea,
or Gulf of Mexico. Many of these remain over the ocean; however, about five hurricanes strike the United States coastline every
three years. Of these five, two will be major hurricanes, category
3 or greater on the Saffir-Simpson Hurricane Scale. . . .

In the eastern Pacific, hurricanes start forming by mid-May. In
the Atlantic, Caribbean, and Gulf of Mexico, hurricane season
starts in June. For the United States, peak hurricane threat exists
from mid-August to late October although the official hurricane
season extends through November. Over other parts of the world,
such as the western Pacific, hurricanes can occur year-round. . . .

# Who Is at Risk?

*Coastal areas and barrier islands.* All Atlantic and Gulf coastal areas
are subject to hurricanes or tropical storms. Although rarely
struck by hurricanes, parts of the Southwest United States and
Pacific Coast suffer heavy rains and floods each year from the
remnants of hurricanes spawned off Mexico. Islands, such as
Hawaii, Guam, American Samoa, and Puerto Rico, are also subject to hurricanes. During 1993, Guam was battered by five typhoons. Hurricane Iniki struck the island of Kauai, Hawaii, on
September 11, 1992, resulting in $1.8 billion damage.

Due to the limited number of evacuation routes, barrier islands are especially vulnerable to hurricanes. People on barrier
islands and in vulnerable coastal areas may be asked by local officials to evacuate well in advance of a hurricane landfall. If you
are asked to evacuate, do so IMMEDIATELY!

*Inland areas.* Hurricanes affect inland areas with high winds, floods, and tornadoes. Listen carefully to local authorities to determine what threats you can expect and take the necessary precautions to protect yourself, your family, and your property.

• *Camille*, August 14–22, 1969: 27 inches of rain in Virginia caused severe flash flooding.

• *Agnes*, June 14–22, 1972: Devastating floods from North Carolina to New York produced many record-breaking river crests. The storm generated 15 tornadoes in Florida and 2 in Georgia.

• *Hugo*, September 10–22, 1989: Wind gusts reached nearly 100 mph as far inland as Charlotte, North Carolina. Hugo sustained hurricane-strength winds until shortly after it passed west of Charlotte.

• *Andrew*, August 16–28, 1992: Damage in the United States is estimated at $25 billion, making Andrew the most expensive hurricane in United States history. Wind gusts in south Florida were estimated to be at least 175 mph.

# The U.S. Hurricane Problem

*Population growth.* The United States has a significant hurricane problem. Our shorelines attract large numbers of people. From Maine to Texas, our coastline is filled with new homes, condominium towers, and cities built on sand waiting for the next storm to threaten its residents and their dreams.

There are now some 45 million permanent residents along the hurricane-prone coastline, and the population is still growing. The most rapid growth has been in the sunbelt from Texas through the Carolinas. Florida, where hurricanes are most frequent, leads the nation in new residents. In addition to the permanent residents, the holiday, weekend, and vacation populations swell in some coastal areas 10- to 100-fold.

A large portion of the coastal areas with high population densities are subject to the inundation from the hurricane's storm surge that historically has caused the greatest loss of life and extreme property damage.

*Perception of risk.* Over the past several years, the warning system has provided adequate time for people on the barrier islands and the immediate coastline to move inland when hurricanes have threatened. However, it is becoming more difficult to evacuate people from the barrier islands and other coastal areas because roads have not kept pace with the rapid population growth.

The problem is further compounded by the fact that 80 to 90 percent of the population now living in hurricane-prone areas have never experienced the core of a "major" hurricane. Many of these people have been through weaker storms. The result is a false impression of a hurricane's damage potential. This often leads to complacency and delayed actions which could result in the loss of many lives.

*Frequency of hurricanes.* During the 70's and 80's, major hurricanes striking the United States were less frequent than the previous three decades. With the tremendous increase in population along the high-risk areas of our shorelines, we may not fare as well in the future. This will be especially true when hurricane activity inevitably returns to the frequencies experienced during the 40's through the 60's.

In the final analysis, the only real defense against hurricanes is the informed readiness of your community, your family, and YOU. . . .

# What to Listen For

NOAA [National Oceanic and Atmospheric Administration] Weather Radio is the best means to receive warnings from the National Weather Service. The National Weather Service continuously broadcasts updated hurricane advisories that can be received by NOAA Weather Radios sold in many stores. The average range is 40 miles, depending on topography. Your National Weather Service recommends purchasing a radio that has both a battery backup and a tone-alert feature which automatically alerts you when a watch or warning is issued.

- *Tropical storm watch*: Tropical storm conditions are possible in the specified area of the watch, usually within 36 hours.
- *Tropical storm warning*: Tropical storm conditions are expected in the specified area of the warning, usually within 24 hours.
- *Hurricane watch*: Hurricane conditions are possible in the specified area of the watch, usually within 36 hours. During a hurricane watch, prepare to take immediate action to protect your family and property in case a hurricane warning is issued.
- *Hurricane warning*: Hurricane conditions are expected in the specified area of the warning, usually within 24 hours. Complete all storm preparations and evacuate if directed by local officials.
- *Short term watches and warnings*: These provide detailed in-

formation on specific hurricane threats, such as tornadoes, floods, and high winds.

Information for local decision makers [includes the following]:

- The *public advisory*—issued by the National Hurricane Center provides critical hurricane warning and forecast information.
- The *marine advisory*—issued by the National Hurricane Center provides detailed hurricane track and wind field information.
- The *tropical cyclone update*—issued by the National Hurricane Center highlights significant changes in a hurricane that occur between advisories.
- *Probabilities of hurricane/tropical storm conditions*—provide a measure of the forecast track accuracy. The probabilities have no relation to tropical cyclone intensity.
- *Hurricane local statements*—issued by local National Weather Service offices give greater detail on how the storm will impact your area.

All of the above information must be used to make an informed decision on your risk and what actions should be taken. Remember to listen to your local official's recommendations and to NOAA Weather Radio for the latest hurricane information.

## Personal and Community Preparedness

*Before the hurricane season . . .*

- Know the hurricane risks in your area.
- Learn safe routes inland.
- Learn location of official shelters.
- Ensure that enough non-perishable food and water supplies are on hand.
- Obtain and store materials, such as plywood, necessary to properly secure your home.
- Clear loose and clogged rain gutters and downspouts.
- Keep trees and shrubbery trimmed.
- Review your insurance policy.

Individuals with special needs or others requiring more information should contact their local National Weather Service office, emergency management office, or American Red Cross chapter.

*When in a watch area . . .*

- Frequently listen to radio, TV, or NOAA Weather Radio for official bulletins of the storm's progress.

- Fuel and service family vehicles.
- Inspect and secure mobile home tie downs.
- Prepare to cover all window and door openings with shutters or other shielding materials.
- Check batteries and stock up on canned food, first-aid supplies, drinking water, and medications.
- Prepare to bring inside lawn furniture and other loose, lightweight objects, such as garbage cans, garden tools, etc.
- Have on hand an extra supply of cash.

*Plan to evacuate if you . . .*

- Live in a mobile home. They are unsafe in high winds, no matter how well fastened to the ground.
- Live on the coastline, an offshore island, or near a river or a flood plain.
- Live in a high-rise. Hurricane winds are stronger at higher elevations.

*When in a warning area . . .*

- Closely monitor radio, TV, or NOAA Weather Radio for official bulletins.
- Complete preparation activities, such as putting up storm shutters, storing loose objects, etc.
- Follow instructions issued by local officials. Leave immediately if told to do so!
- If evacuating, leave early (if possible, in daylight). Stay with friends or relatives, at a low-rise inland hotel/motel, or go to a predesignated public shelter outside a flood zone.
- Leave mobile homes in any case.
- Notify neighbors and a family member outside of the warned area of your evacuation plans.
- Put food and water out for a pet if you cannot take it with you. Public health regulations do not allow pets in public shelters, nor do most hotels/motels allow them.

*What to bring to a shelter:* first-aid kit; medicine; baby food and diapers; cards, games, books; toiletries; battery-powered radio; flashlight (one per person); extra batteries; blankets or sleeping bags; identification, valuable papers (insurance), and cash.

*Reminder! If you ARE told to leave, do so immediately!*

# During the Storm

*If staying in a home . . .*

Only stay in a home if you have NOT been ordered to leave.

Stay inside a well constructed building. In structures, such as a home, examine the building and plan in advance what you will do if winds become strong. Strong winds can produce deadly missiles and structural failure.

- Turn refrigerator to maximum cold and open only when necessary.
- Turn off utilities if told to do so by authorities.
- Turn off propane tanks.
- Unplug small appliances.
- Fill bathtub and large containers with water for sanitary purposes.

*If winds become strong . . .*

- Stay away from windows and doors even if they are covered. Take refuge in a small interior room, closet, or hallway.
- Close all interior doors. Secure and brace external doors.
- If you are in a two-story house, go to an interior first-floor room, such as a bathroom or closet.
- If you are in a multiple-story building and away from the water, go to the first or second floors and take refuge in the halls or other interior rooms away from windows.
- Lie on the floor under a table or another sturdy object.

*Be alert for . . .*

- Tornadoes which often are spawned by hurricanes.
- The calm "eye" of the storm. After the eye passes, the winds will change direction and quickly return to hurricane force.

*After the storm . . .*

- Keep listening to radio, TV, or NOAA Weather Radio.
- Wait until an area is declared safe before entering.
- Roads may be closed for your protection. If you come upon a barricade or a flooded road, turn around and go another way!
- Avoid weakened bridges and washed out roads. Do not drive into flooded areas.
- Stay on firm ground. Moving water only 6 inches deep can sweep you off your feet. Standing water may be electrically charged from underground or downed power lines.
- Check gas, water, and electrical lines and appliances for damage.
- Do not drink or prepare food with tap water until you are certain it is not contaminated.
- Avoid using candles and other open flames indoors. Use a

flashlight to inspect for damage.
- Use the telephone to report life-threatening emergencies only.
- Be especially cautious if using a chainsaw to cut fallen trees. . . .

## Preparing a Family Disaster Plan

Families should be prepared for all hazards that could affect their area. NOAA's National Weather Service, the Federal Emergency Management Agency, and the American Red Cross urge every family to develop a family disaster plan.

Where will your family be when disaster strikes? They could be anywhere: at work, at school, or in the car. How will you find each other? Will you know if your children are safe? Disaster may force you to evacuate your neighborhood or confine you to your home. What would you do if basic services water, gas, electricity or telephones were cut off?

*Follow these basic steps to develop a family disaster plan . . .*

1. *Gather information about hazards.* Contact your local National Weather Service office, emergency management office, and American Red Cross chapter. Find out what type of disasters could occur and how you should respond. Learn your community's warning signals and evacuation plans.

2. *Meet with your family to create a plan.* Discuss the information you have gathered. Pick two places to meet: a spot outside your home for an emergency, such as fire, and a place away from your neighborhood in case you can't return home. Choose an out-of-state friend as your "family check-in contact" for everyone to call if the family gets separated. Discuss what you would do if advised to evacuate.

3. *Implement your plan.*
   - Post emergency telephone numbers by phones;
   - Install safety features in your house, such as smoke detectors and fire extinguishers;
   - Inspect your home for potential hazards (such as items that can move, fall, break, or catch fire) and correct them;
   - Have your family learn basic safety measures, such as CPR and first aid; how to use a fire extinguisher; and how and when to turn off water, gas, and electricity in your home;
   - Teach children how and when to call 911 or your local Emergency Medical Services number;

- Keep enough supplies in your home to meet your needs for at least three days. Assemble a disaster supplies kit with items you may need in case of an evacuation. Store these supplies in sturdy, easy-to-carry containers, such as backpacks or duffle bags. Keep important family documents in a waterproof container. Keep a smaller disaster supplies kit in the trunk of your car.

4. *A disaster supplies kit should include:*
   - A 3-day supply of water (one gallon per person per day) and food that won't spoil
   - one change of clothing and footwear per person
   - one blanket or sleeping bag per person
   - a first-aid kit, including prescription medicines
   - emergency tools, including a battery-powered NOAA Weather Radio and a portable radio, flashlight, and plenty of extra batteries
   - an extra set of car keys and a credit card or cash
   - special items for infant, elderly, or disabled family members.
   - *Practice and maintain your plan.* Ask questions to make sure your family remembers meeting places, phone numbers, and safety rules. Conduct drills. Test your smoke detectors monthly and change the batteries two times each year. Test and recharge your fire extinguisher(s) according to manufacturer's instructions. Replace stored water and food every 6 months. Contact your local National Weather Service office, American Red Cross chapter, or local office of emergency management for a copy of "Your Family Disaster Plan."

# The Saffir-Simpson Hurricane Intensity Scale

| Category | Barometric Pressure (mb)* | Wind Speed (mph) | Storm Surge | Damage |
|---|---|---|---|---|
| 1 "weak" | 980 or more | 74–95 | 3–5 feet | shrubbery and small trees uprooted; mobile homes damaged |
| 2 "moderate" | 981–965 | 96–110 | 6–8 feet | some damage to roofs, windows, and doors; considerable pier and marina damage; some coastal flooding |
| 3 "strong" | 964–945 | 111–130 | 9–12 feet | large trees damaged; mobile homes destroyed; serious coastal flooding; structural damage to buildings |
| 4 "extreme" | 944–920 | 131–155 | 13–18 feet | most trees, shrubs and signs blown down; serious damage to houses; beach erosion; required coastal evacuation; flooding for several miles inland |
| 5 "cata-strophic" | 920 or less | 155 or more | over 18 feet | all trees and signs blown down; severe damage to or destruction of buildings and homes; major flooding; required evacuation of population within 5 to 10 miles of coastline |

Developed in the early 1970s by consulting engineer Herbert Saffir and meteorologist Robert Simpson.

*Normal barometric pressure at sea level is 1013 millibars (mb).

# The Fifteen Most Deadly Atlantic Hurricanes Since 1492

| Rank | Name/Location | Year | Deaths |
|------|---------------|------|--------|
| 1 | "Great Hurricane," Martinique and Barbados | 1780 | 22,000 |
| 2 | "Mitch," Central America | 1998 | 10,000+ |
| 3 | Galveston, Texas | 1900 | 8,000+ |
| 4 | "Fifi," Honduras | 1974 | 8,000+ |
| 5 | "Flora," Haiti and Cuba | 1963 | 8,000 |
| 6 | Dominican Republic | 1930 | 2,000–8,000 |
| 7 | Guadeloupe | 1776 | 6,000 |
| 8 | Newfoundland Banks | 1775 | 4,000 |
| 9 | Puerto Rico and Carolinas | 1899 | 3,500 |
| 10 | Martinique, Guadeloupe, Puerto Rico, and Florida | 1928 | 3,400 |
| 11 | Cayman Islands, Jamaica, and Cuba | 1932 | 3,000 |
| 12 | Central Atlantic (offshore) | 1782 | 3,000 |
| 13 | Martinique | 1813 | 3,000 |
| 14 | El Salvador and Honduras | 1934 | 3,000 |
| 15 | Western Cuba | 1791 | 3,000 |

# The Fifteen Most Deadly U.S. Hurricanes Since 1900

| Rank | Name/Location | Year | Category | Deaths |
|---|---|---|---|---|
| 1 | Galveston, Texas | 1900 | 4 | 8,000+ |
| 2 | Lake Okeechobee, Florida | 1928 | 4 | 1,836 |
| 3 | Florida Keys and Texas | 1919 | 4 | 600+ |
| 4 | New England | 1938 | 3 | 600 |
| 5 | Florida Keys | 1935 | 5 | 408 |
| 6 | "Audrey," Louisiana and Texas | 1957 | 4 | 390 |
| 7 | Northeastern United States | 1944 | 3 | 390 |
| 8 | Grand Isle, Louisiana | 1909 | 4 | 350 |
| 9 | New Orleans, Louisiana | 1915 | 4 | 275 |
| 10 | Northeastern Texas | 1915 | 4 | 275 |
| 11 | "Camille," Mississippi and Louisiana | 1969 | 5 | 256 |
| 12 | Mississippi, Alabama, and Miami and Pensacola, Florida | 1926 | 4 | 243 |
| 13 | "Diane," Northeastern United States | 1955 | 1 | 184 |
| 14 | Southeastern Florida | 1906 | 2 | 164 |
| 15 | Mississippi, Alabama, and Florida Panhandle | 1906 | 3 | 134 |

**advisory:** Official information released by tropical storm warning centers describing all active tropical cyclone watches and warnings along with details concerning storm location, intensity, and movement, and any safety precautions that should be taken.

**anemometer:** An instrument used to measure wind speed.

**Beaufort wind scale:** The scale used to define wind speed, created by British admiral Francis Beaufort in 1806 to describe sea winds.

**cloud seeding:** Inseminating clouds with dry ice or other particles to modify the clouds' natural formation, which usually increases precipitation. In the 1960s, scientists attempted to reduce hurricane intensity through cloud seeding.

**condensation:** The process by which water vapor is converted to water, releasing heat.

**convection:** The transfer of heat upward into the atmosphere that frequently creates thunderstorms.

**cyclone:** A low-pressure area in which winds rotate in a counterclockwise direction in the Northern Hemisphere and in a clockwise direction in the Southern Hemisphere.

**dropsonde:** An instrument package dropped from "hurricane hunter" aircraft and lowered to the ocean with a parachute. Dropsondes measure wind speed, temperature, humidity, and barometric pressure inside hurricanes.

**dropwindsonde:** A dropsonde that uses satellite tracking to measure hurricane data at different altitudes.

**El Niño:** From the Spanish word for "boy child," the name given to a periodic warming of the ocean in the eastern Pacific near the equator. The phenomenon tends to increase tropical cyclone activity in the eastern Pacific while inhibiting the development of hurricanes in the Atlantic.

**eye:** The circular area of relatively light winds at the center of a hurricane.

**eye wall:** A ring of thunderstorms with powerful winds that surround the eye of a hurricane.

**hurricane:** A tropical cyclone with sustained winds of seventy-four or more miles per hour.

**hurricane hunters:** The fleet of U.S. Air Force and National Oceanic and Atmospheric Administration planes that fly into hurricanes to determine intensity and direction.

**hurricane warning:** An alert declaring that a hurricane is expected to hit a coastline in twenty-four hours or less.

**hurricane watch:** An alert declaring that a coastline may be hit by a hurricane in thirty-six hours or less.

**landfall:** When and where the center of a hurricane crosses from the ocean onto land.

**La Niña:** From the Spanish word for "girl child," the name given to a periodic cooling of the eastern Pacific near the equator. La Niña tends to inhibit tropical cyclone activity in the eastern Pacific while providing more favorable conditions for the development of Caribbean and Atlantic hurricanes.

**low-pressure area:** An area where winds flow around a central point in a counterclockwise manner in the Northern Hemisphere and where the net movement of air is upward.

**major hurricane:** A hurricane with sustained winds of more than 110 miles per hour.

**meteorologist:** An individual who studies and/or forecasts the weather; requires a university degree in meteorology or a degree in math or physics with the appropriate meteorology classes.

**paleotempestology:** The study of prehistoric hurricanes.

**peak gust:** Highest wind of a one- to three-second duration.

**precipitation:** Liquid or frozen drops of moisture that fall from the atmosphere.

**scud clouds:** Low, dark, patchy, swiftly moving clouds.

**shear:** The difference in the speeds or directions of winds at different altitudes. "Low vertical shear"—when winds blow in the same direction up through the troposphere—provides favorable conditions for the development of hurricanes. "High shear"—winds blowing in opposite directions at different levels of the atmosphere—inhibits the development of hurricanes.

**spiral bands:** Curving streams of clouds and precipitation that circle inward toward the center of a hurricane. Also known as "feeder bands."

**storm surge:** An abnormal rise in sea level resulting from the massive, wind-driven ocean wave that develops during a hurricane. When the hurricane makes landfall, the storm surge causes major coastal flooding.

**sustained wind:** In the United States, the average speed of wind for the duration of one minute. (Internationally, the ten-minute average wind speed.)

**tornado:** A powerful, twisting windstorm that begins in the air currents of a thunderhead and touches the ground. A hurricane may spawn tornadoes as the storm moves inland.

**tropical cyclone:** A cyclone that forms over a tropical ocean with a center that is warmer than the surrounding atmosphere.

**tropical depression:** A tropical cyclone with sustained winds of less than thirty-nine miles per hour.

**tropical disturbance:** An area of tropical thunderstorms that lasts for more than twenty-four hours—sometimes the earliest stage of a hurricane.

**tropical storm:** A tropical cyclone with sustained winds of thirty-nine to seventy-three miles per hour.

**tropical wave:** An area of disturbed weather that develops over Africa and travels westward across the Atlantic Ocean, sometimes spawning Atlantic hurricanes.

**tropics:** The region of the earth that extends from latitude 23.5 degrees north to latitude 23.5 degrees south.

**troposphere:** The lower level of the earth's atmosphere, up to about 50,000 feet, in which the temperature decreases with altitude.

**typhoon:** The regional term for a hurricane in the western Pacific north of the equator.

**vortex:** A circular flow of air around a low-pressure center.

## FOR FURTHER RESEARCH

### Books

Patricia Bellis Bixel, *Galveston and the 1900 Storm: Catastrophe and Catalyst.* Austin: University of Texas Press, 2000.

Gordon Chaplin, *Dark Wind.* New York: Atlantic Monthly Press, 1999.

Pete Davies, *Inside the Hurricane: Face to Face with Nature's Deadliest Storms.* New York: Henry Holt, 2000.

James B. Elsner, *Hurricanes of the North Atlantic: Climate and Society.* New York: Oxford University Press, 1999.

David E. Fisher, *The Scariest Place on Earth: Eye to Eye with Hurricanes.* New York: Random House, 1994.

Patrick J. Fitzpatrick, *Natural Disasters, Hurricanes: A Reference Handbook.* Santa Barbara, CA: ABC-CLIO, 1999.

Jonathan D. Kahl, *National Audubon Society First Field Guide: Weather.* New York: Scholastic, 1998.

Erik Larson, *Isaac's Storm.* New York: Crown, 1999.

David Longshore, *Encyclopedia of Hurricanes, Typhoons, and Cyclones.* New York: Facts On File, 1998.

Michael H. Magil and Barbara G. Levine, *The Amateur Meteorologist.* New York: Franklin Watts, 1993.

Andrew Robinson, *Earthshock: Hurricanes, Volcanoes, Earthquakes, Tornadoes, and Other Forces of Nature.* New York: Thames & Hudson, 2002.

Jeffrey O. Rosenfeld, *Eye of the Storm: Inside the World's Deadliest Hurricanes, Tornadoes, and Blizzards.* New York: Plenum Trade, 1999.

Bob Sheets and Jack Williams, *Hurricane Watch: Forecasting the Deadliest Storms on Earth.* New York: Vintage Books, 2001.

# Periodicals

Jay Barnes, "Creatures in the Storm," *Weatherwise*, September/October 1998.

Patricia Barnes-Svarney, "Awful Agnes," *Weatherwise*, May/June 2002.

Lennart Bengtsson, "Hurricane Threats," *Science*, July 20, 2001.

Mace Bentley and Steve Horstmeyer, "Hurricane Legacies," *Weatherwise*, September 1999.

Barbie Bischof, "Ocean Tantrums," *Natural History*, September 1999.

Nancy Anne Dawe, "Hugo's Legacy," *American Forests*, Autumn 1999.

Jan Deblieu, "Whirling Hurricanes," *Audubon*, September 1999.

Margaret Eastman, "The Great Hurricane," *American Heritage*, September 1998.

*Economist*, "Eye on the Storm," February 26, 2000.

Paul R. Epstein, "Climate and Health," *Science*, July 16, 1999.

Pico Iyer, "Trail of Tears and Anguish: A Killer Cyclone Rips Across the Bay of Bengal, Taking at Least 15,000 Lives," *Time*, June 10, 1985.

Steven S. Lapham, "What's in a Name? A Whirlwind Tour of the World!" *Social Education*, May 2001.

Nick Middleton, "Coming to Blows," *Geographical*, October 2000.

Mark I. Pinsky, "Pricey Predictions," *Quill*, January/February 1999.

Carl Posey, "Hurricanes: Reaping the Whirlwind," *Omni*, March 1994.

Jill Sieracki, "Survivors of the Storm," *Good Housekeeping*, August 2002.

Gary Smith, "Hugo Dealt a Blow to This Charlestonian's Manhood," *Sports Illustrated*, October 23, 1989.

Gary Smith and Lynn Johnson, "In the Eye of the Storm: A Year Later Hurricane Hugo's Water Is Gone, but Life Is Still Pretty Muddy," *Life*, September 1990.

Richard Symanski, "Honduras: When the Saints Arrive," *Geographical Review*, October 1998.

Louis Werner, "Great Storms of the Four Winds: Scientists in a New Field Are Studying Hurricanes of Prehistory to Uncover Clues . . . ," *Americas (English Edition)*, September/ October 2002.

A.R. Williams, "After the Deluge: Central America's Storm of the Century," *National Geographic*, November 1999.

## Websites

Federal Emergency Management Agency (FEMA), www.fema. gov. FEMA offers brochures on home and community hurricane preparedness as well as a news archive on past and current weather disasters.

National Climatic Data Center, www.ncdc.noaa.gov. The center's website has the world's largest archive of weather data, including details on all significant U.S. hurricanes since 1900.

National Hurricane Center, www.nhc.noaa.gov. The center maintains a continuous watch on tropical cyclones in the Atlantic, Caribbean, Gulf of Mexico, and eastern Pacific regions from May 15 to November 30. It prepares advisories, hurricane watches, and hurricane warnings for the public. The website provides information on tropical weather outlooks, hurricane history, and hurricane research.

National Oceanic and Atmospheric Administration (NOAA), www.noaa.gov. NOAA provides general information on hurricanes, access to all U.S. hurricane watches and hurricane warnings, and links to other websites on climate and weather.

National Weather Service, http://iwin.nws.noaa.gov. The National Weather Service is an interactive weather information network that provides all national weather service home pages as well as live computer data broadcasts via satellite, radio, and the Internet.

Storm Prediction Center, www.spc.noaa.gov. The center's website has a summary of all severe weather of the previous day and official statistics for the past several years.

USAToday Weather Page, http://asp.usatoday.com/weather/weatherfront.asp. This site offers a searchable archive on hurricane history, safety, and preparedness, as well as photos, satellite images, and seasonal outlooks.

Weather Channel, www.weather.com. The Weather Channel allows you to find your local weather forecast and provides weather-related videos for viewing.

# INDEX